*The
Poetry
Circus*

The Poetry Circus

by *STANTON A. COBLENTZ*

HAWTHORN BOOKS, INC.
PUBLISHERS
NEW YORK

CONTENTS

The
Poetry
Circus

INTRODUCTION

All through my life, poetry has been for me a joy and a wonder, a pilot and an inspiration. Ever since the days of lonely adolescence, when it provided consolation and companionship, it has enriched my world with treasures beyond reckoning. But the poetry that has called to me has been a poetry of singing and ringing lines, of skylarks and a wild west wind, of lovers and midnight trysts, of mountains and stars and the towers of Camelot. It has been a poetry of all the dreams, the hopes and aspirations that make up life, all life's delights and sorrows, its searches and achievements and despairs, and its passionate reaching toward other worlds. Most of all, it has been a poetry of nobility and music, which has made life seem more meaningful and has given glimpses of universes beyond the senses and of truths beyond logic.

But this poetry, which has characterized all the great English-speaking bards until our own century, is part of our experience no longer. Not that we refuse lip service to all the masters. Not that some recent survivors of the old school, such as Robert Frost and Walter de la Mare, have not received considerable praise. But as far as the present generation is concerned, we in America and, to a large extent, our contemporaries in England have abandoned the very type of poetry that gave wings to Chaucer, Spenser, Shakespeare, and every other outstanding poet up to and including the earlier Yeats. In place of the mellifluous lines of Shelley, Keats, and Poe, we have

9

work that is deliberately raucous and consciously shocking. In place of the resounding utterances and profound meanings of Milton and Wordsworth, we have the apotheosis of triviality. All that was hailed as poetry yesterday has been abandoned today; literally, the nonpoets and the antipoets have taken over.

In such an atmosphere, the youth of this generation will not enjoy the lift or the inspiration that came to me in adolescence. Amid flat, hard objectivities portrayed in cold and toneless lines, he will find no impulse to look beyond horizons; he will discover no answer to his questionings, his doubts, his craving for insight. I myself, for all my lifelong love of poetry, would not have been a devotee of the art had I grown to manhood in the present period; the pretentious ramblings of the moderns would have given me no satisfaction; almost of necessity I would have turned to prose, doubtless without realizing that I had been denied my birthright. If I were the only member of a species, this would mean little. But there must be thousands who, if given the chance, would react as I did to poetry. These, however, have had the misfortune to be born into a world where it is unconventional to write metrically or to let imagination or emotion have the free play that made possible such works as *A Midsummer Night's Dream, Lycidas, Kubla Khan,* and *Elegy in a Country Churchyard.* Because I feel that we are depriving our potential poets and poetry lovers of something precious, and depriving them without their knowledge and beyond their power to help themselves, I feel that the situation desperately calls for action.

Let me not be misunderstood. I do not oppose progress or experimentation. I am not wedded to the idea of rhymed poetry, even if I do believe that rhyme may at times be an invaluable asset. Nor am I a partisan of any particular technique or metrical school, though I maintain that the beat of a regular rhythm—which has marked Western poetry ever since Homer—cannot be abandoned without altering the nature of poetry. Progress, I realize, must come in all fields, but this does not necessarily mean denial of the past: the axioms of Euclid need not be relinquished just because they were first propounded long ago, or because new insights have come to later mathematicians. In the same way, in poetry, we may indeed experiment, just as poets have long done, but we should not sweep away our foundations. Our present verse writers, however, have gone beyond experimentation to revolution; and thus, in losing sight of all previous principles, they have driven out poetry itself.

Yet this situation, portentous as it is, has not generally been brought to light. In England some of the older writers—for example, Lord Dunsany in occasional articles, and Gilbert Murray in *The Classical Tradition in Poetry* (1927)—have struck out stanchly against the forces of disruption. A more recent writer, David Holbrook, in a book on Dylan Thomas, has proclaimed that he does not find in contemporary poetry the most satisfying of the qualities that appealed to him in the poems of the past. And Russell Hope Robbins (an Englishman by birth and education but later an American resident) tells us in his persuasive *The T. S. Eliot Myth:*

> The current Eliot vogue is no mystery; the Eliot problem . . . is the logical reflection of present-day decadence. Those who shrug off, or are themselves caught up in, this trend should at least realize what they are heading toward: the suppression of all creative activities, ultimately including their own, and the abandonment of the mainstream tradition of culture and enlightenment.

Despite such rare strong words, there have been few broad and revealing analyses since the appearance in 1919 of John Livingston Lowes' *Convention and Revolt in Poetry.* The situation, as I see it, is nothing short of scandalous. Although poetry, as a living voice, has almost ceased to be heard, no protests are raised. Is it that no one cares? I cannot believe so. Or is it that everyone is so cowed by authority that none dares to say that black is not white? Again, I hesitate to believe so. But the facts are there, and the facts speak plainly and tell us that the pseudopoets possess the field. And since no general survey of these facts has ever been made, it has occurred to me to write the present book, not to advance any case of my own, but to serve as an advocate of poetry—poetry, the modern stepchild of the arts, which may yet be restored to its place among the great creative and inspirational forces if we will but open our eyes and observe what is happening.

I

THE PLODDING MUSE

A number of years ago an American expatriate, locked in an insane asylum while under indictment for treason, was awarded a prize of $1,000 by the Fellows of the Library of Congress. The excuse for this recognition was a book of poems entitled *Pisan Cantos,* which the prize committee adjudged the best of the year. Here are two lines:

> one tanka entitled the shadow
> babao, or the hawk's wing

In much the same spirit are other characteristic lines, such as

> Pisa, in the 23rd year of the effort in sight of the tower
> and till was hung yesterday
> for murder and rape with trimmings   plus cholkis
>   plus mythology, thought he was Zeus ram or another one
>   Hey Snag wots in the bibl'?

This work by Ezra Pound, long heralded as one of America's outstanding poets, may seem extreme. Yet compared with certain other recent offerings it appears almost conservative. Take this, by an equally acclaimed leader of twentieth-century American poetry:

> &(all during the

> dropsin

king god my sic
kly a thingish o crashdis
appearing con ter fusion ror collap
sing thatthis is whichwhat yell itfulls o
f cringewiltdroolery i

If this excerpt were an isolated example, one might dismiss it with
a gasp or a yawn. But whole books are filled with offerings in the
same style as this one from E. E. Cummings' *Xaipe, Seventy-one
Poems*. Take this beginning of another nameless "poem" from the
same volume:

tw

o o
ld
o

nce upo

n
a(
n

o mo

Insanity? Or mere tomfoolery? The charitable reader may prefer
to call it the latter. Yet, tomfoolery or not, sputterings of this sort
have been greeted with widespread critical applause, and at times
with considerable financial returns. Thus *Xaipe,* though it follows
much the same technique throughout, some years ago gained Cummings a $5,000 award from the Academy of American Poets. Nor has
this been the author's only high honor. In 1957 he received the
coveted Bollingen Prize for his "gift of natural wit and lyric imagination." And he has been regarded so seriously that during his lifetime he was the subject of an extensive biography and critical

14

appraisal, Charles Norman's *The Magic-Maker E. E. Cummings.*
As a further example of the work of this "magic-maker," this man
of "natural wit and lyric imagination," observe the following, from
Number 221 of his *Collected Poems:*

of
   THuNdeRB
     loSSo!M iN
-visiblya mongban(gedfrag-
ment ssky?wha tm)eani ngl(essNessUn
rolli)ngl yS troll s(who leO v erd)oma insCol
Lide.!high
      n , o ; w :
          theraIncomIng

Apologists for Cummings have defended his practices with the
claim that he builds upon Greek models—just as if Greek poetry
were not admirably patterned, with a "classical restraint" and without excesses. Cummings' writing, however, is not the important
thing. The important thing is that it is taken seriously by most
critics, and has rarely been berated even for its extreme aberrations.
The important thing is that a flouter of standards, whose typical
work is not only beneath poetry but beneath prose and actually casts
contempt upon poetry, has been widely anthologized, has been made
a subject of study in schools, and has provoked few critical voices
to assert the obvious—that he brays rather than sings. When such a
new unanimity, such an evident cowing of critical opinion, is possible, what has happened to poetry?

But let us go on. Cummings, after all, may be held to be the single
representative of a species. His uniqueness, which consists in the
main of typographical and linguistic distortions, has indeed had
imitators, but hardly puts him in the mainstream of modern verse
writing. Let us take examples somewhat nearer to the average. Here
is a passage from a writer perhaps not less esteemed than Cummings
himself:

In these non-committal, personal-impersonal expressions of
appearance,
the eye knows what to skip;
the physiognomy of conduct must not reveal the skeleton;
'a setting must not have the air of being one',
yet with X-ray-like inquisitive intensity upon it, the surfaces
go back;
the interfering fringes of expression are but a stain on what
stands out,
there is neither up nor down to it . . .

In this typical excerpt from Marianne Moore's *Collected Poems,*
there are no typographical displacements, no efforts to confuse or
impress the reader by freakish arrangements of letters or punctuation marks. And the selection, even if not a model of clarity, is by
no means unintelligible. But to say that a work is not freakish, and
that it is intelligible, is by no means to proclaim that it is poetry. In
these lines, as in virtually all the offerings of Miss Moore, the poetry
is difficult if not impossible to discover. Consider how the passage
would read without the author's line divisions:

In these non-committal, personal-impersonal expressions of
appearance, the eye knows what to skip. The physiognomy of
conduct must not reveal the skeleton; 'a setting must not have
the air of being one.' Yet with X-ray-like inquisitive intensity
upon it, the surfaces go back. The interfering fringes of expression are but a stain on what stands out, there is neither up
nor down to it.

I have, admittedly, made some slight adjustments in the punctuation. Yet who that came upon this passage, printed as just above,
would see in it anything but a rather heavy prose? Are we then to
suppose that punctuation and line divisions are the distinguishing
marks of poetry?

No matter what examples of Miss Moore's work we choose, the
results are the same. Take the following, also from *Collected Poems.*

Again I have transcribed the work into prose form, though with no changes in punctuation:

Strong and slippery, built for the midnight grass-party confronted by four cats, he sleeps his time away—the detached first claw on the foreleg, which corresponds to the thumb, retracted to its tip; the small tuft of fronds or katydid-legs above each eye, still numbering the units in each group; the shadbones regularly set about the mouth, to droop or rise in unison like a porcupine's quills—motionless . . .

Here too it is hard to see anything beyond a somewhat ponderous prose. So again we ask: Can the printed form of a work be a sufficient claim to the title of poetry?

Yet offerings of exactly this nature—offerings no less difficult to distinguish from an uninspired, academic prose—have won Marianne Moore a plethora of awards, including the Helen Haire Levinson Prize, the Dial Award, and the Ernest Hartsock Memorial Prize for 1935; the Shelley Memorial Award of 1940; the Contemporary Poetry Patrons' Prize of 1944; a Guggenheim Memorial Fellowship in 1945; the National Institute of Arts and Letters Awards for 1946 and 1953; the Bollingen Prize, the National Book Award of the American Book Publishers' Council, and the Pulitzer Prize in Poetry, all in 1952; and the National Institute of Arts and Letters Gold Medal for Poetry in 1953.

At this point, let me make it plain that this discussion does not chiefly involve the question of free verse versus conventional poetry, nor of the older techniques versus the new. Work in the traditional forms, as many of us know, can be quite as dull and prosy as the most vapid outpourings of the rebels. For example, the following by Archibald MacLeish is not lifted far above the prose level by the accoutrements of rhyme and a regular meter:

Quite unexpectedly as Vasserot
The armless ambidextrian was lighting
A match between his great and second toe

And Ralph the lion was engaged in biting
The neck of Madame Sossman while the drum
Pointed, and Teeny was about to cough . . .

And these lines of light verse by Ogden Nash, though they also use rhyme and meter, say nothing that could not be stated just about as effectively in straight prose:

Lots of truisms don't have to be repeated but there is one that
    has got to be,
Which is that it is much nicer to be happy than it is not to be,
And I shall even add to it by stating unequivocally and with-
    out restraint
That you are much happier when you are happy than when
    you ain't.

Keeping in mind the mood, spirit, and subject matter of the writing rather than the technique, glance at this example:

He walks out of the village. The road lowers into a hollow which villagers call the Borough, though it contains only a farm, a stream where small boys go newting, and four medieval town houses which drop plaster in the frosts of winter, and which a decade will dismantle. . . .

Is this a passage out of a contemporary novel? Not at all. Divided into nine lines, it is the beginning of a poem in Donald Hall's recent book, *A Roof of Tiger Lilies*. Again we have to ask: Is the test of poetry a mere typographical arrangement on a page?

Or consider the following, on the theme of grandparents:

They're altogether otherworldly now, those adults champing for their ritual Sunday spin to pharmacist and five-and-ten in Brockton. Back in my throw-away and shaggy span of adolescence, Grandpa still waves his stick like a policeman; Grandmother, like a Mohammedan, still wears her thick lavender mourning and touring veil . . .

18

If you encountered this in a current piece of fiction, would anything about it suggest that you were reading poetry? Yet, printed as poetry, it is the beginning of a selection in Robert Lowell's book of verse, *Life Studies*.

Here once more, as in a multitude of cases, appearances are all that tell you whether the author claims to be writing poetry or prose. Not only that, but if the printed appearance were changed, the reader would be uncertain whether the piece was intended as poetry or prose. Let me present some further examples by way of a test. I have selected a number of passages, half of them originally offered as prose, and half as poetry; and I shall reproduce some as they first appeared, but shall take liberties with others, giving verse the physical appearance of prose, or prose the physical appearance of verse. I shall ask the reader to decide for himself how each was first printed, and then to turn to the end of the chapter to identify the passages. Doubtless some readers will recognize certain excerpts, which to that extent will limit the test; and clues may be provided by mannerisms in certain of the poems. In any event, one must remember that haphazard guesses would on the average be 50 percent correct.

A further fact should be made plain. In picking these selections, I have necessarily avoided the more eccentric specimens of verse— necessarily because the reader would instantly recognize that they are too bad to pass as prose.

First, then, for some examples in prose form. Of the following two, one originally appeared as poetry:

If, on account of the political situation, there are quite a number of homes without roofs, and men lying about in the countryside neither drunk nor asleep; if all sailings have been cancelled until further notice, it is unwise to say much in letters, and if under the subnormal temperatures prevailing, the two sexes are at present the weak and the strong, that is not at all unusual for the time of the year.   (1)

Life tore at them with its heartbreak. They could not escape the hurt of it by selfish refuge in the gluttonies of brain and body. They saw, and steeled themselves to see, clear-eyed and unafraid. Nor were they afflicted by some strange myopia. They all saw the same thing. They all agreed upon what they saw. (2)

Here is a second pair, one of which was first published as poetry, while the other makes no poetic pretensions. This time I reproduce one with the looks of verse:

> Pale morning steals in
> with the new day's
> set of unfulfilled wants . . .
> hunger for a smile . . . or a letter
> . . . or merely a bowl of
> warming broth.
> Shelter, food, friendship . . . with
> these a man has a place
> among people and a meaning
> to his life. The essentials
> for living can be guaranteed. (3)

The clear, brown eyes, kindly and alert, with 20–20 vision, give confident regard to the passing world through R. K. Lambert and Company lenses framed in gold. His soul, however, is all his own: Arndt Brothers necktie and hat (with feather) supply a touch of youth. (4)

Now for two more offerings, of which again one originally appeared as poetry:

There are four vibrators, the world's exactest clocks; and these quartz time-pieces that tell time-intervals to other clocks, these workless clocks work well; independently the same, kept in the 40° Bell laboratory time-vault. Checked by a comparator with Arlington, they punctualize the "radio, cinema," and "presse"—a group the Giradoux truth-bureau of hoped-for accuracy has termed "instruments of truth." (5)

There are many turret clocks in various parts of Europe, and a limited number in England. The largest of them is the Strasbourg clock of 1547. It aims at showing the movements of the earth and stars as well as the time, also the seasons, epochs of the year, moral emblems and the life of man; it was restored in 1842. Some of these clocks contain large figures which strike the hours. (6)

By way of variety, I present two further selections in the garb of verse:

All, all is blue in the calm—
Save the low land under your feet, which you almost forget,
Since it seems only as a green flake
Afloat in the liquid eternity of day.
Then slowly, caressingly, irresistibly,
The witchery of the Infinite grows upon you:
Out of Time and Space you begin to dream with open eyes—
To drift into delicious oblivion of facts—
To forget the past, the present, the substantial—
To comprehend nothing but the existence of that infinite
    Blue Ghost . . . (7)

The Atlantic is a stormy moat, and the Mediterranean,
The blue pool in the old garden,
More than five thousand years has drunk sacrifice
Of ships and blood and shrines in the sun; but here the Pacific:
The ships, planes, wars are perfectly irrelevant.
Neither our present blood-feuds with the brave dwarfs
Nor any future world-quarrel of westering

And eastering man, the bloody migrations, greed of power,
    battle-falcons,
Are a mote of dust in the great scale-pan.   (8)

The next two I give in the shape of prose, though one was not originally so printed:

> There is, it seems to us, at best only a limited value in the knowledge derived from experience. The knowledge imposes a pattern, and falsifies, for the pattern is new in every moment and every moment is a new and shocking evaluation of all we have been. We are only undecided of that which, deceiving, can no longer harm.   (9)

> Truth has a nature of its own to which our individual thinking must conform or fail to grasp it. By our making, we can neither make nor alter truth; we may come to recognize it, but we cannot invent it; and its nature is unaffected by the circumstances that at a particular time and under certain conditions it is acknowledged by us.   (10)

It would be intriguing to go on indefinitely, but I must confine myself to two final illustrations. Both are from a well-known American magazine, and I take liberties with the original form of one:

> I am a scientist, a toxologist, to be precise. Often I treat a rabbit in its ear vein. I then observe its spasms and rapid pulse, measuring with care its movements and metabolism, kill it and note a petechial hemorrhage, lungs. Quite routine, of course. What's a rabbit, or a hundred, to human life?   (11)

> . . . I volunteered to go to Lancaster, Pennsylvania, to pick up some "local color." I did not anticipate that the "colors" I would find in the capital of the Pennsylvania Dutch country would be exclusively white and gray. But the time I picked

for my visit was March 20, the day of one of the worst storms in Lancastrian history, and the local colors were the white of snow and the gray of slush. (12)

As these quotations suggest, the distinction between poetry and prose has largely broken down. And if this distinction has broken down, if in many cases it designates nothing more than the difference between even and uneven columns of print, what right has poetry to exist at all? What better right than a man has to dress in feminine apparel and call himself a woman? Has poetry not, for all practical purposes, actually ceased to exist? Is there not here a misrepresentation, a fraud? Is there not a flouting of poetry, of its meaning, its nature, its mission? Is not a hoax being perpetrated upon the public? Is not one of the greatest of the arts being betrayed by its critics and practitioners?

Key to quotations: (1) W. H. Auden, from "For the Time Being." (2) Jack London, from introduction to "The Cry for Justice," in *Jack London, American Rebel,* p. 526. (3) From advertisement of the Columbian National Life Insurance Company, in *The Atlantic.* (4) Kenneth Fearing, from "Portrait II," in *100 American Poems,* edited by Selden Rodman. (5) Marianne Moore, from "Four Quartz Crystal Clocks," in *Collected Poems.* (6) *Encyclopaedia Britannica,* 14th ed., Vol. 5, p. 838. (7) Lafcadio Hearn, in his story "Chita," from *The Selected Writings of Lafcadio Hearn,* p. 141. (8) Robinson Jeffers, from "The Eye," in Oscar Williams' *The Pocket Book of Modern Verse.* (9) T. S. Eliot, in *Four Quartets.* (10) *Encyclopaedia Britannica,* 14th ed., Vol. 13, p. 465. (11) From "The Toxologist," poem by Leigh Van Valen, in *The Saturday Review.* (12) From Pyke Johnson Jr.'s prose in "Trade Winds," in *The Saturday Review.*

II

HOW TO WRITE
A MODERN POEM

To understand just what is implied by the current tendency to confuse poetry and prose, we must glance at the history of poetry as far back as classical Greece and Rome.

Poetry has meant the swing of the majestic hexameter and the rousing chants "of arms and men" of Virgil and Homer. Poetry has meant the passion of high drama and the soaring of a vast imagination in Euripides, Sophocles, and Shakespeare. Poetry has meant music and love, storm and ecstasy, the marshaling of great ideas in a Milton, a Goethe, a Wordsworth, the singing surge of emotional experience in a Burns, a Heine, a Keats, a Shelley, the nobility of dreams and of aspiration, "the light that never was on sea or land," the suggestiveness of sunsets fading behind lonely hills, the terror and glory of ocean expanses, the daintiness at the heart of a daisy, and the magnificence and mystery at the heart of man. Poetry has been prayer and beauty, wonder and illumination; but above all this and beyond all this it has been the evocation of things not seen or known, the clutching at lights and meanings beyond the doors of the senses. This, and not the technique that has given it effect, has principally set poetry off from prose.

But this sets poetry off from prose no longer—not, at least, in the writing of the self-styled moderns. How and why has the tremendous change come about? Perhaps we will find one answer, out of many, if we ask how poems today come to be written.

It is important to note that we have, in the world of verse, an approach to multiple production. This does not mean that there are, as has been loosely claimed, millions of poets in contemporary America, nor that any poet produces by methods of the assembly line. Nevertheless, the number of verse writers and would-be verse writers, as distinguished from poets, is beyond calculation. A thorough search might not reveal a verse writer in every cabbage patch, garage, chain store, warehouse, office, or kitchen; but the astonishing fact is that many cabbage patches, garages, chain stores, warehouses, offices, and kitchens do contain followers of the Muse. I myself, from lifelong experience and most of all from twenty-seven years as editor of a poetry magazine, realize how numerous are such aspiring poets, and with what unremitting floods of offerings they invade the editorial offices. I have known such hopefuls in many occupations: on the police force, in the post office, on California fruit ranches, and in a railroad switch tower. I have seen one as a street singer, one as a title examiner, one as a worker in a mattress store, one as a probation officer, one as a noted ornithologist, and one as an eminent bridge builder. I have observed others as physicians, as newspapermen, as pupils in the grade schools, as college students and college teachers, as itinerants, as old-age pensioners, and as retired men and women of independent means. There is only one point in common that I have ever detected in this motley multitude: the desire to write poetry and to be recognized as poets.

In quality of attainment, according to my observation, they differ as widely as in occupation and in life status. Here and there some promising talent, some augury of brilliant accomplishment, flashes before the startled eye. The great majority, however, are flat, insipid, hopelessly uninspired, hopelessly without suggestions of poetry. Yet the great majority, unfortunately, do more than the exceptional few to set the standards. Their attitudes toward poetry go far in determining the trend of the work offered to editors; and even though the bulk of such work is necessarily rejected, there is a residue that finds its way into print and consequently has its effect in setting the current style.

Let us therefore observe how such work comes to be written. The cases given below, while the details are admittedly imaginary, are based upon actual observation.

Clearly, only two courses are open to the aspirant who wishes to be known as a poet. The first, which is so unpopular nowadays as to be hardly worth mentioning, is to take the long, hard road, to act as would a man who wished to master law, medicine, or engineering: to study the subject from the foundations, to familiarize oneself with the work of the great builders of the past, and to give years to study, training, and practice. The poet who sets out on such a course, obviously, must be not without talent if he is to succeed; he must be prepared to work laboriously and long, with the prospect of little or no reward. But how many a writer nowadays, whatever his ability, will give himself to such a monastic routine, especially if he sees prospects of recognition by quicker and easier means? True, the quicker and easier means will never lead to the creation of an "Eve of St. Agnes" or a "Rime of the Ancient Mariner." But even if the poet makes no music for the ages, at least he may hear the music of applause.

And so, rejecting the old, arduous, boresome way, the aspirant sets out to compose a poem. Perhaps, however, he has no idea in mind; he has nothing to say. But does this deter him? Not at all. Since he need not be troubled by old-fogey ideas of rhyme and meter and of a distinction between poetry and prose, he sets out boldly by forgetting everything he has ever heard about poetry and every bit of poetry he has ever read.

Let us say that he is looking out of the window, with nothing whatever in his head, and all he sees is the concrete pavement underneath. Being determined to write a poem, he asks himself: Why not begin with the word "concrete"? But it does not look very original when written on the page in its usual form, and so he divides it, as follows:

Con-
crete

Now there, he tells himself, rubbing his hands together in high self-approval, is the beginning of a poem in the modern style. Of course, poems in one word are not the fashion, so he must think of something else. He sees a lumber truck bumping along in the middle of the street, and this inspires him to write:

> Con-
> crete
> lumber truck bumping in the mid-
> dle of the street.

Ah! he has even produced a rhyme between "crete" and "street," though he didn't mean it and it was not really necessary. At this point he is stuck, and no ideas enter his head for about ten minutes, after which his mind wanders off to a letter which came from his grandmother that morning. Good! This will carry the poem along! Not that the letter had anything to do with the lumber truck, or with the concrete either. But, of course, he has risen far above the old hackneyed, conventional ideas of sequence and relevancy. Therefore he hastily jots down:

> Grandmother Arbuthnot! when you wrote up-
> braiding me for my tardiness in
> not answering your last letter
> dated november 17
> 1964

Now he is stuck again. But once more the concrete and the lumber truck come to the rescue, and so the poet puts them in again:

> concrete . . . concrete . . . con-
> crete
> lumber truck . . . lumber truck . . . lum-
> ber truck bumping in the mid-
> dle of the street.

So there he has his finished poem! He sits back and surveys it proudly. True, it says nothing in particular, and what it does say is a little mixed up. But this does not bother him, for he is not obsessed by any of the "old-hat" traditional notions. He is content to think that the reader, being unable to decide just what is meant, will assume that the author has a profound connection in mind between the lumber truck and his grandmother. And if the reader cannot be sure just what that connection is, he will blame his own dullness, and will never for a moment admit that he does not see the point. Then, too, if any small-minded, old-fashioned critic should complain that the poem is on about the same level of inspiration as the lumber truck, the poet will stick his nose high in the air and say that he has passed far beyond the ancient Milton-Byron-Tennyson sort of stuff. He is a member of the emancipated school. He believes in modern methods.

If you suppose this case to be merely fictional, look at one or two specimens of actual verse writing. Here, for example, is the beginning of "Christmas Poem for the 4th Friend" by Murray Mednick, in the current avant-garde magazine *Pogammoggan*:

> red from the roses of Eden the sun/
> 5th avenue descends/
> it is not the bomb yet
> although "once you get through
> > it's palms up
> > & all you see is the Lord"
> spare me matadors now
> but those goddamned hungry suits
> must be disentangled/

And here, moving in the same direction, is the opening of "Saturday Sermons," by Lucy Lapp, in another modernist verse magazine, *Imagi:*

> Malleable or resilient the self must sometime
> assume (virtue-like) a particular rigidity
> as of interior-armour
> > or like soul

suddenly resident in the stiff bones.

Religious or lay submission to
     permanencies of incidents
     perpetuities of concurring fates
(as the sapling bending forever in a forever-high wind)
produces a logical if ugly curvature,
martyrdom can be warping . . .

Admittedly, not all "emancipated" verse writers—certainly not even a majority—desire to imitate the style of either of the above. Let us therefore turn to a conjectured poet who prefers a "middle of the road" course, avoiding extremism, but also avoiding rules and technique, rhyme and meter, and all the exacting methods of the English-speaking poets from Chaucer to Masefield. Let us further assume that, unlike the author of the piece about the lumber truck, the writer sets out with an impression or an idea to convey. Suppose, for instance, that he has visited the zoo and been moved by the zebra. He hopes to communicate what he has felt, but never thinks of uttering himself except as in a prose essay. Therefore he begins:

The zebra is a curious beast.
He is dressed all his life in stripes like a convict.
He is a child of Africa,
where he roams the veld in herds of many hundreds,
a cousin to the horse,
though he cannot be tamed like the broncho.

These are the writer's thoughts, just as they come to him, without any attempt to refine them, to choose among them, or to make them stand out with memorable expressions. The trouble is not only that the lines do not sing, but that they transmit no more of an idea or a mood than any prose article; they lack the spirit of poetry. "The zebra is a curious beast." This could have been said in a child's introduction to natural history. "He is dressed all his life in stripes like a convict." Conceivably this might be transformed into poetry, but in its present form it merely states the obvious in obvious language. "He is a child of Africa, where he roams the veld in herds of many hundreds." Here is nothing that might not be included in a "Primer of Animal Life." In none of these is there the originality, the suggestiveness, the appeal to the mind and imagination of Blake's celebrated lines:

> Tiger! Tiger! burning bright
> In the forests of the night,
> What immortal hand or eye
> Could frame thy fearful symmetry?

Nor is there the individual approach, the feeling, the observation, or the pity of Burns in his poem "To a Mouse":

> Wee, sleekit, cow'rin, tim'rous beastie,
> Oh, what a panic's in thy breastie!
> Thou need na start awa sae hasty,
> Wi' bickerin brattle!
> I wad be laith to rin an' chase thee
> Wi' murd'rin pattle!

Unquestionably Blake and Burns were aided by rhyme and a regular rhythm, but the basic distinction goes deeper; the basic distinction is one of mental approach. The delineator of the zebra remains outside his subject; Burns, on the other hand, identifies himself with the feelings of the mouse, while Blake evokes the vast and solemn question of the creative hand behind the visible image. The writer on the zebra, however, is following in the footsteps of thousands; he is faithful to the contemporary creed, which stresses objectivity. And because he has not risen beyond objectivity, he has not produced the mood of poetry.

Let us go on to another example. Suppose that a writer is concerned about matters of war and peace and troubled at the state of the contemporary world. Certain thoughts come to him, and he sits down to embody them in a poem. He begins with the reflection that

The peace-makers and the war-makers in the modern world
are at opposite poles.

At this point he hesitates; it comes to him that the phrase "at opposite poles" is trite and must be rejected. Hence he changes the line
to read:

The peace-makers and the war-makers in the modern world
are at the opposite ends of a conjunction.

This may be a little vague and somewhat hard to figure out, perhaps even contradictory, but no one will say it is trite. One can be
sure that no writer ever used this phrase before. Well content with
himself, the poet goes on to write:

They are as far apart as midnight from noon or April from
November.

Having written this, the poet gasps and groans—he has fallen
again into the same old error of triteness. Midnight and noon, April
and November may have been well enough for Wordsworth, Longfellow, and the other ancients, but now they are out of date. Accordingly, after a little brow-scratching, the poet alters the line to read:

They are as far apart as a yawn from vertigo, or an aspersion
from a hypotenuse.

Here, again, he has avoided triteness. Here, again, he has introduced fresh and original images. It never occurs to him that there
might be anything incongruous about mixing yawns and vertigo
and a hypotenuse with matters of war and peace.

Better pleased with himself than ever, the poet goes on to write:

Every nation,
isolated in its own house,
seeks to wall out all other nations.

Of course, this will not do. The writer has not developed his individual speech, his own idiom. He must transmute the lines into something more novel, more distinctive. It takes considerable further cogitation before he has accomplished the next step:

Every nation
in the isolation of its own libido
seeks to cro-Magnonize all others with the psychology of the
    alter ego.

The poet reads, and admires. What originality! What genius! True, he has only the haziest idea of the meaning of "libido" and "alter ego," and cannot find the verb "cro-Magnonize" in the dictionary. But this only makes him the more original. He has produced something sophisticated, something distinguished in the modern manner. By this time, of course, he has completely forgotten that he ever had anything to say as to war and peace.

He has, likewise, lost sight of the great models of the past: the rousing war poetry of *The Iliad* and *The Song of Roland;* the martial scenes in *Macbeth,* "Arm, arm, and out!" . . . "My voice is in my sword," "Fear not, till Birnam Wood/Do come to Dunsinane"; the sonorous tones of Byron, "Battle's magnificently stern array!"; and the ironic tones of Southey in "The Battle of Blenheim":

"And everybody praised the Duke
    Who this great fight did win."
"But what good came of it at last?"
    Quoth little Peterkin.
"Why, that I cannot tell," said he;
"But 'twas a famous victory."

The differences between our conjectured modern and his great predecessors are of course many; but one point stands out. And this is that the modern, in pursuance of the current cult, is trying to air his own ego; while Shakespeare, Byron, and the others sought to convey something beyond themselves. In other words, they placed

32

communication first, and for that reason they were great communicators. But the modern has given us something which, however it may please the coteries, could not conceivably be of universal and enduring interest. The modern, perhaps unconsciously, has cheated —and has not given us poetry at all.

III

STRUTTERS, SWAGGERERS,
AND GESTICULATORS

Just as the greatest man may be the most unassuming, so the most
accomplished art may be the least pretentious. Having real merit, it
need not pose or perform contortions to show proofs of merit. This,
of course, is as true of poetry as of the other arts. Note Wordsworth's
well-known lines:

> She dwelt among the untrodden ways
>   Beside the springs of Dove,
> A Maid whom there were few to praise
>   And very few to love:
>
> A violet by a mossy stone,
>   Half hidden from the eye!
> Fair as a star, when only one
>   Is shining in the sky.
>
> She lived unknown, and few could know
>   When Lucy ceased to be;
> But she is in her grave, and oh
>   The difference to me!

Here there is not a single striking or original word or phrase, not
a word or phrase that a modern critic might not call hackneyed or

overworked. Yet no single word or phrase needs to be striking. For the whole is striking enough.

The same is true of other outstanding work, such as these celebrated lines by Ernest Dowson:

> They are not long, the weeping and the laughter,
> Love and desire and hate;
> I think they have no portion in us after
> We pass the gate.
>
> They are not long, the days of wine and roses:
> Out of a misty dream
> Our path emerges for a while, then closes
> Within a dream.

Again there is not a word that stands out. There is not a pose nor a gesture. It is the completed product that counts rather than the part. And the completed product will not be helped by acrobatics.

But acrobatics, as we have noted, are precisely what we often have nowadays. We are treated to a performance rather than to a poem. The poet struts, swaggers, and gesticulates; he is interested in manner rather than in substance; all that he tries to convey is his own personality. And to accomplish this end, he may resort to a variety of devices.

One of the most obvious of these devices is what we have seen in E. E. Cummings: to take liberties with the printed work, to hack up the words, to abandon punctuation, as in several examples I have quoted, or to run the words together, as in these lines from Terence Heywood's *How Smoke Gets into the Air:*

> Samsonseeingstone,
> Shakespearesynopting-lovechains-easily-smasht,
> Beethovenhearingthroughanemptyear

On the other hand, a poet occasionally tries to shock by a monstrous excess of punctuation—which is somewhat as if a chef seasoned his broth by indiscriminately pouring in all the condiments in the kitchen. An illustration is a piece by José Garcia Villa, published some years ago in *Poetry* of Chicago. I quote the first stanza:

> And,Theseus,then,Minotaur
> Coherence,and,severance,
> By,the,seven,locks,of,strictness: by,diamond-law
> Bolt,me,more.   Bolt,Him,more.
> What,brightfall,is,this—I,see,Him.
> In,the,eyes,of,a,Tear.

To read this is like running a hurdle race. After virtually every word, one is stopped short by an obstacle. But the obstacles are purely artificial, and can have only one reason—to shock and startle the reader. In every line, the author is posing and gesticulating. Poetry is his last consideration. If there were any poetry in the above, which I doubt, it would be lost to sight amid the obstructions of the punctuation, just as Dowson's moving lines would be obscured and ruined if printed as follows:

> They,are,not,long,the,weeping,and,the,laughter,
> Love,and,desire,and,hate.

Another frequent method of attack upon words is to arrange them in a geometrical form, which, in extreme cases, may be that of a pyramid or a diamond or even of some strange and fabulous-looking monster. A less fantastic example, but one that illustrates the trend, is this from "400-meter free style" in Maxine W. Kumin's book, *Halfway:*

> THE GUN full swing the swimmer catapults and cracks
>
>   s
>
>   i
>
>   x
>
> feet   away   onto   that   perfect   glass   he   catches   at
> a
> n
> d

36

throws behind him scoop after scoop cunningly moving

t
h
e

water back to move him forward. Thrift is his wonderful

s

e

c

And so on for nearly three pages. But what relation have such gymnastics to poetry?

Another example—not so bizarre, but hardly less affected—is this from Louis MacNeice's "Prayer Before Birth":

> I am not yet born: O fill me
> With strength against those who would freeze my
>   humanity, would dragoon me into a lethal automaton,
>   would make me a cog in a machine, a thing with
>   one face, a thing, and against all those
>   who would dissipate my entirety, would
>   blow me like thistledown hither and
>   thither or hither and thither
>   like water held in the
>   hands would spill me.

By concentrating on the diagonal line, the reader is hypnotized into forgetting the poetry, if it exists. I think it fair to state that here, as in all cases where geometry enters, poetry departs.

But the chief means used by the strutters and gesticulators are, of course, not mathematical. One expedient, employed by Ezra Pound in his *Cantos* and by T. S. Eliot in *The Waste Land,* is to impress the reader with little known or unknown foreign phrases, which would seem merely pompous or affected if not actually funny in prose. A less ponderous device is that of the English poet John Wain in his sixteen-line "Poem in Words of One Syllable." Other methods, however, are less obvious. If our common English speech can be tormented to mean what it has never meant before, if it can be twisted into forms and connotations never known on heaven or earth, then what inexhaustible opportunities for the shocker! Take, for example, this line by Jack Lindeman in *New World Writing 19:* "The Marseillaise, like a shark's tooth." Or this by Daisy Aldan in *The Destruction of Cathedrals:* "7x7 drunken triangles/Cavort like slick puppets." Or this by David Shapiro in *Harper's Magazine:* "The ocean is full of flowers that betray me/Because your unhappiness has a hospital in it." Or this by Paul Blackburn in *The New American Poetry: 1945–1960:* "emasculate his god and general manager in charge of/blow his earth up." Or, finally, this by Ray Bremster, also in *The New American Poetry:*

> your heaps of slick and apathetic succor
> transvestite my human animal until I walk
> with knuckles on the ground, my Einstein essence
> split by prehistoric gobs of eyed typography

As in the above, the normal relationships of things may be reversed. The sky may cease to be blue, and become green or purple; light may become black, and darkness white; up may become down, and down may become up, and long may become short, and anything may become anything else that it has never been before in nature or in the imagination of man. Cheeses may become turtles, worms may become rainbows, and curbstones clouds; slime may become exquisite, and roses disgusting. And, of course, poetry may become prose. Since anything that may shock and even horrify the reader may serve a purpose, the writer may go out of his way to tread upon traditional concepts and time-honored sensibilities, as in some of the passages already quoted, or as when a writer in a poetry magazine a few years ago referred to "the snout of God," and when Jack Spicer, in *The New American Poetry,* tells us that "God feeds on God. God's goodness is/A black and blinding cannibal with sunny teeth/That only eats itself." And if this ugliness is nearer to profanation than to poetry, it has abundant company in the many modern attempts to evoke the hideous and to confuse hideousness

and beauty. Thus Karl Shapiro has a much anthologized poem on "The Fly," beginning

> O hideous little bat, the size of snot.

It is hard to believe that the author could not have found a less loathsome figure—had he wished a less loathsome figure.

In the same vein is this from Carol Bergé in *Four Young Lady Poets:*

> i talk filth and energy
> pissing at them the vacant horror
> of my lofts and days
> passed from my pennsylvania mother
> like dung or philosophy . . .

If this is poetry, then green cheese is art.

Further examples, likewise illustrating the extraordinary modern theory that the purpose of poetry is to shock, can be cited almost *ad infinitum.* Consider Auden's

> Kicking his mother until she has let go of his soul
> Has given him a healthy appetite.

Observe MacNeice's

> Throwing our dreams and guts in people's faces.

Note Robert Lowell's

> When the Pulitzers showered on some dope
> or screw who flushed our dry mouths out with soap.

Or glance at this, by Kenneth Patchen, in *Golden Goose Chap Book,* #6:

Do you know what I am say?
Have you thought of love today?
Behind this familiar scenery of words
the fear-stained placenta
the muchronated cowlknife
the enchorial puddercap
the dissentient conglutination
the dagglesome crassitude
the spool-mouthed gaddement
the ruck-souled concinnity
the sperm-gummed ankylosis
the winnowrimous scissility . . .
the bull-rigged hartalor . . .

What, one may ask, is the author attempting? To write poetry? Or to exhibit himself in a circus?

And if he is exhibiting himself in a circus, why are such displays commonly mistaken for poetry? Is there not something topsy-turvy in our standards when such a prosy and posing verbal stunt can pass as the advanced poetry of our age?

But, after all, why be concerned with these sputterings? Does not such work sign its own death warrant? Ah, yes! But this is to express only half a truth. It is not as if Patchen's contemptuous sort of tampering with poetry were limited to a single author. While the individual example may soon fade from view, the species remains, like thistles that survive in the seed; its influence upon the rising generation will linger. Youth accepts the models placed before it; and if the models are those of the cellar and the cesspool, then the cellar and the cesspool will be imitated, perhaps admired. From personal observation, I can testify to this truth: as editor of a poetry magazine, though one which published no avant-garde work, I received a constant stream of submissions in imitation of Cummings, Pound, Eliot, and the other gods of the day; and occasional submissions in the same vein still reach my desk. If this were not proof enough, abundant evidence would be provided by the published

work of the younger generation. Here, for example, is the opening
stanza of David R. Slavitt's "Cerberus" (*Poets of Today,* VIII):

The thunderhead of the dogday's night
fringed with ermine, mooncrossing slowly,
bearing its ancient, rere regardant,
breaks the formation, hovering lovely
with a havoc cry and a shower of might . . .

Here is the beginning of "The Hairbrush," from Paul Roche's
The Rank Obstinacy of Things:

Each little freshet of bristles
pulling at the air
Drilled staccato
into a barrage of bristles
hitting reality.

The chopped rain
of its held and imbricated hair
Dentilled with sprouting shadows
crowding, carding
And winnowing the space around it
Baffling the space within it
Broadcasting its small colleges of
bristles . . .

And here is an excerpt from "Moses Rock," in William Gibson's
Winter Crook:

My faucets open like mouths in love but our mains
Cough in a deathguggle rust
And the tanks rot on our stilts: how can we sing
In our alley of must

And gossip in lickspittle eddies, souls like newspapers
Daft in a gutter of airs,
Where the finicky tips of my fellows pick at my sleeve
And I at theirs

41

Note that this employs both rhyme and meter but is no more poetic for that reason. A junk pile does not flower even when sprayed with the perfume of violets.

Still another example is "Egghead," from Ted Hughes' *The Hawk in the Rain,* which won the First Publication Award of Poetry Center of New York. I quote the conclusion:

> Dewdrop frailty
> Must stop the looming mouth of the earth with a pin-
> Point cipher, with a blank-stare courtesy
> Confront it and preen,
>
> Spurn it much under
> His foot-clutch, and, opposing his eye's flea-red
> Fly-catching fervency to the whelm of the sun,
> Trumpet his own ear dead.

I confess that I have been unable to discover what this means, or to divine its relationship to poetry. All that I can see is an awkward effort to strike a pose.

But shall we point an accusing finger at younger and less-known poets who but follow in the tracks of age or reputation? What shall we say, for example, of a widely published American, John Berryman, whose "From Homage to Mistress Bradstreet" (in Lord David Cecil and Allen Tate's *Modern Verse in English 1900–1950*) is constructed of stanzas such as the following?

> Winter than summer worse, that first, like a file
> on a quick, or the poison suck of a thrilled tooth;
> and still we may unpack.
> Wolves & storms among, uncouth
> board-pieces, boxes, barrels vanish, grow
> houses, rise. Motes that hop in sunlight slow
> indoors, and I am Ruth
> away: open my mouth, my eyes wet: I would smile . . .

A more celebrated writer, Dylan Thomas, has provided some work so strained, clumsy, and turgid that the name poetry can be applied to it only as an undeserved courtesy. Take this, from "January, 1939":

> In the sniffed and poured snow on the tip of the tongue of
>   the year
> That clouts the spittle like bubbles with broken rooms,
> An enamoured man alone by the twigs of his eyes, two fires,
> Camped in the drug-white shower of nerves and food,
> Savours the lick of the times through a deadly wood of hair
> In a wind that plucked a goose,
> Nor ever, as the wild tongue breaks its tombs,
> Rounds to look at the red, wagged root.

And observe this, from Thomas' offering unassumingly entitled "Poem":

> When I woke, the town spoke.
> Birds and clocks and cross bells
> Dinned aside the coiling crowd,
> The reptile profligates in a flame,
> Spoilers and pokers of sleep,
> The next-door sea dispelled
> Frogs and satans and woman-luck,
> While a man outside with a billhook,
> Up to his head in his blood,
> Cutting the morning off,
> The warm-veined double of Time
> And his scarving beard from a book,
> Slashed down the last snake as though
> It were a wand or subtle bough,
> Its tongue peeled in the wrap of a leaf.

These pieces go beyond obscurity to pretense. They gesticulate, but they convey nothing to the reader; they leave him only chaff and straw to carry away with him. Consequently, they fail as poetry. But what when such pieces are elevated as idols for the younger generation? What when, in schools and libraries and in the salons of the sophisticated, they are exalted as the standard, the guide, the key-note of the future?

So strongly has the cult of appearances prevailed that expression has largely been subordinated to manner; the poetic realities have been lost to view in the preoccupation with surfaces. And one result is that, in many cases, a modern poem can be read with equal effect from the bottom up. Here, for example, is an excerpt from E. E. Cummings' 95 *Poems:*

> forgetting me, remember me
> (when time from time shall set us free)
> and in a mystery to be
>
> remember seek (forgetting find)
> whatever mind may comprehend,
> in time of all sweet things beyond . . .

Was this originally printed as above? No, for I have taken liberties with the lines, reversing their order, so that the last is now first and the first last. But who would notice the difference?

Next, to return to Dylan Thomas, consider this from "Do not Go Gentle into That Good Night":

> Rage, rage against the dying of the light.
> Do not go gentle into that good night.
> Curse, bless me now with your fierce tears, I pray.
> And you, my father, there on the sad height,
> Rage, rage against the dying of the light.
> Blind eyes could blaze like meteors and be gay.
> Grave men, near death, who see with blinding sight
>
> Do not go gentle into that good night.

This, as a poem, is much superior to the preceding quotations. But who would know, upon reading it, that the lines are printed in reverse order?

Now observe the following:

They that take the bribe shall perish by the bribe,
Dying of dry rot, ending in asylums,
A curse to children, a charge on the state,
But still their fears and frenzies infect us;
Drug nor isolation will cure this cancer:
It is now or never, the hour of the knife,
The break with the past, the major operation.

Again the selection—from C. Day Lewis' "Consider These, For We Have Condemned Them"—is printed with the lines in reverse order.

And the same is the case with this from Archibald MacLeish's "Hypocrite Auteur":

> Invent the age! Invent the metaphor!
> Turn round the actual air,
> Poets, deserted by the world before.
> Still knocks at silence to be understood
> The ignorant blood
> That is its glass.
> Still stares into the summer grass
> The allegory of the flesh and bone.
> The metaphor still struggles in the stone,
> Earth turns us still toward the rising east,
> The journey of our history has not ceased.

Let me cite two final examples, which should be considered together:

(1) But to have done instead of not doing
         This is not vanity
     To have, with decency, knocked
     That a Blunt should open
         To have gathered from the air a live tradition
     Or from a fine eye the unconquered flame
     That is not vanity.
         Here error is all in the not alone.

(2) Pull down thy vanity,
      In scaled invention or true artistry,
      Learn of the green world what can be thy place
      Pull down thy vanity, I say pull down.
      Made courage, or made order, or made grace,
      Pull down thy vanity, it is not man.
      The ant's a centaur in his dragon world.

Both are from the *Cantos* of Ezra Pound. The first is here printed without change; the second is in reverse order.

I have other examples before me, but these should suffice. I will confess to having altered the punctuation of some of the selections, adding or removing a comma or period here and there to permit an uninterrupted flow. But I submit that, though an accidental instance or two might conceivably be found, it would be impossible to go to the classic English poets and discover a succession of pieces that read as well from the bottom as from the top.

This, therefore, leaves us to wonder as to the direction taken by the new movement in poetry. Are its practitioners standing on their feet or on their heads?

IV

THE MUSIC OF THE BUZZ SAW

Most things in nature have rhythm: the twittering of birds and the murmuring of bees, the movements of the tides and the billowing of meadow grass beneath a wind, the gliding flight of the gull and the long succession of ocean waves breaking upon a beach, the alternation of the seasons and the progression from day to night and from night to day. In the human body also there is rhythm, not only in the beating of the heart and the circulation of the blood and the everlasting intake and outpouring of breath but likewise in the motions of walking, in the regular swinging of the arms and legs. Even human speech, in its more inspired and exalted moments, has an unpatterned and yet at times a pronounced rhythm.

What more natural, therefore, than that rhythm should enter into poetry? And when we find it to be dominant, should we regard it as a mere technical device or as something basic to man's being, just as it is basic in many phenomena of nature?

The fact is that, more than any other clearly defined attribute, rhythm has distinguished poetry from the day of *The Odyssey* to that of Yeats' *The Wanderings of Oisin*. One can go further and say that rhythm has distinguished poetry ever since its primitive beginnings in folk songs and ballads, when it was timed to the chant of the spoken word. But even when it came to be composed chiefly for the pages of books, rhythm remained of prime importance. He who reads a poem to himself, and reads it with full appreciation and enjoyment, repeats in his mind the ring and flow of the lines and savors the color and the reiterated beat of the words, by which the movement and the sublimities of thought and feeling impress themselves upon him and linger in his memory. Thus it may truly be said that, even in the silence of the printed page, poems do and must sing. There are undoubtedly those today who are insensitive to singing effects and seek to impose their tone deafness upon others as a great new discovery of the age; but they are in a class with Aesop's tailless fox who tried to induce his relations to cut off their tails.

Glance for a moment at a few of the many uses of rhythm in English poetry. Rhythm has stood out in the rhymeless forms employed by Longfellow in *Evangeline* and other long narratives. Rhythm has been at the heart of blank verse with its Shakespearean power and splendor and its Miltonic majesties. Rhythm has underlain all the great lyrics of the English language, beginning with the simplicities of the early ballads such as "Chevy Chase":

> God prosper long our noble king,
> Our liffes and safetyes all;
> A woefull hunting once there did
> In Chevy-Chace befall.

Rhythm has been a leading characteristic of the best modern poems, as in the singing rush of Masefield's "The Seekers":

> Friends and loves we have none, nor wealth nor blessed abode,
> But the hope of the City of God at the other end of the road.

Rhythm has powerfully aided one of the most notable recent Americans, Edwin Arlington Robinson, in *The Valley of the Shadow:*

> There were faces to remember in the Valley of the Shadow,
> There were faces unregarded, there were faces to forget . . .

It is important to keep such lines in mind when one turns to the newer school and seeks to understand what it has done with the most fundamental of poetic tools. Unfortunately, it often does not matter whether you glance at recent rhymed or unrhymed poetry; your findings as to rhythm are likely to be much the same in either case. Take the work of Merrill Moore, a physician-poet who, before his death in 1957 at the age of fifty-four, earned considerable repute for compositions which he labeled "sonnets"—Louis Untermeyer, in the introduction to one of Moore's books, makes the incredible estimate that he turned out forty thousand in the course of his not overlong life. Here is the beginning of one, from *Poems of American Life:*

> I am tired of seeing my face; I am fatigued
> At shaving my face, considerably indisposed
> At washing my face, my body, combing my hair,
> And of having it cut about once every two weeks,
> Of brushing my teeth and using dental floss,
> Seeing the dentist and having cavities filled,
> Seeing a doctor and therefor being billed . . .

And this is from *Verse-Diary of a Psychiatrist:*

> Some women are the way they are because
> They have always had to steal things from the jaws
> Of men, throughout their lives, and never had
> Much peace of mind or choice of good or bad
> But only this prescribed or that coerced,
> Statutory chattels from the first.

Note that the first composition is unrhymed except for the last two lines, while the second has rhyme throughout. Note also that some lines, such as "Some women are the way they are because" and "Much peace of mind or choice of good or bad," are technically capable of scansion yet fall far short of the ringing effects of good rhythm—effects that only the most unresponsive could fail to feel in "Full many a glorious morning have I seen/Flatter the mountain-tops with sovereign eye," or "The tumult of thy mighty harmonies/ Will take from both a deep autumnal tone," or in a simpler vein:

> O saw ye not fair Innes?
> She's gone into the West,
> To dazzle when the sun is down,
> And rob the world of rest.

By emphasizing the trivial and the unimportant and by expressing themselves in slightly stressed or unstressed petty-sounding syllables, the Merrill Moores bypass rhythm even when they seem to respect the laws of meter. Consequently, their poems may be classified with this, which I have plucked at random from this morning's newspaper:

> A former bartender testified yesterday
> That he was ordered by a Ku Klux Klan
> Superior officer to accompany
> Three other klansmen on a journey which led
> To the slaying of civil rights worker Viola Liuzzo.

Of course, this was not originally printed as above; it appeared as an ordinary news item. But I ask if its rhythm, while somewhat more irregular than Merrill Moore's, is much inferior in its poetic effect. Or is it less poetic in rhythm or in the general impression it conveys than the following, from "In the Junkshop," by the contemporary writer Constance Urdang?

> By sticks and rags, by brass, glass, rust,
> By chairs without backs, by hinges
> Without tables, by stoppers
> Without bottles, by everything broken,
> Cropped, bobbed, docked, truncated—
> Dolls' legs and arms, toy carts without wheels—shawls
> That crumble like ash, old reticules, gloves, lids
> Without boxes, shards, crumbs, splinters . . .

Now consider these lines, from Theodore Roethke's "Reply to a Lady Editor":

Sweet Alice S. Morris, I *am* pleased, of course,
You take the *Times Supplement,* and read its verse,
And know that True Love is more than a Life-Force
—And so like my poem called *Poem.*

You will notice that, despite some irregularities, this is not far from the meter of conventional verse. Yet again the seeming technical conformity does nothing to produce a satisfying rhythmical impression or to elevate the passage toward poetry. The whole would have about the same effect—or perhaps a better effect, because less pretentious and less distracting to the eye—if printed as straight prose.

The modern insensitiveness to rhythm is further demonstrated in Thomas Whitbread's sequence, "Accident." The opening lines follow:

I had ridden the New Haven Railroad so
Many safe times, mostly from Springfield to
New York, that I had not thought any real woe
Could attend its trains greater than being a few
Minutes late. Waiting in Providence, I
Bought a paperback copy of Ray Bradbury's
Dandelion Wine to read in . . .

Let us re-examine this in prose format:

I had ridden the New Haven Railroad so many safe times, mostly from Springfield to New York, that I had not thought any real woe could attend its trains greater than being a few minutes late. Waiting in Providence I bought a paperback copy of Ray Bradbury's *Dandelion Wine* to read in . . .

Compare this with the following:

I first caught sight of him as he sat on the wharf. He was seated on a rather large seaman's chest, painted green and very much battered. He wore gray, his shirt was navy-blue flannel, his necktie a flaring red bandana handkerchief knotted loosely under the ill-fitting lop-sided collar . . .

This excerpt, from Edward Lucas White's short story "The Song of the Sirens," is rhythmically and poetically not at all inferior to Mr. Whitbread's offering, although the author did not represent his work as poetry; indeed, from the point of view of picturesqueness of description, White's passage is conspicuously superior. But the point to note is that the supposed poet has infused no poetry into his work by his use of rhyme and of measured if irregular lines; he has merely supplied a camouflage. Not only is the spirit of poetry not present; we have not even the mechanics of poetry, its decisive stride and its resonant beat.

This statement, however, would be of small importance if it applied only to Mr. Whitbread and a few like him. Unfortunately, the remarks pertain to the vast majority of verse writers who call themselves "modern," whether they claim radical departures in form and method or seem to burn incense at the altars of the old gods. Of most of these it may be said that, in the words of Charles Norman,

> Their strident voices rasp upon the page
> Like leaves scraping dry earth.

It is true that a precedent for rambling, unmetrical, prosy lines was set by Whitman (who, however, was never as extreme in expression and was often more rhythmical than most of the moderns), and his lead was followed by many in this century, including Carl Sandburg, who likewise never descended so far as certain of his successors but set a sufficiently prosy example in lines like

> You come along . . . tearing your shirt . . . yelling about Jesus.
> Where do you get that stuff?

2

Consider Whitman's well-known poem "The Last Invocation":

At the last, tenderly,
From the walls of the powerful fortress'd house,
From the clasp of the knitted locks, from the keep of the well-
  closed doors,
Let me be wafted.

Let me glide noiselessly forth;
With the key of softness unlock the locks—with a whisper,
Set ope the doors O soul.

Tenderly—be not impatient,
(Strong is your hold O mortal flesh,
Strong is your hold O love.)

Here we have neither rhyme nor a prescribed meter; yet here, to my mind, is the rhythm of a completely satisfying poem. Never elsewhere, in all the length of *Leaves of Grass,* has Whitman quite equaled the perfection of these lines, nor have many later *vers-librists* even approached such a blending of meaning and music. Nonetheless, a very few followers of the freer methods have at times drawn near that indeterminate border where prose and poetry meet, while still fewer have given us work that has crossed the border in nobility of utterance and suggestiveness of content no less than in rhythmical quality. Take, for example, Kahlil Gibran, author of *The Prophet.* I do not claim that the cadenced lines of this mystical masterpiece are always distinguishable from a noble prose, yet I do believe that some of its passages give the peculiar satisfaction that springs only from poetry. Consider these lines:

In the stillness of the night I have walked in your streets,
and my spirit has entered your houses,
   And your heart-beats were in my heart, and your breath
was upon my face, and I knew you all.

Ay, I knew your joy and your pain, and in your sleep your dreams were my dreams.
And oftentimes I was among you a lake among the mountains.
I mirrored the summits in you and the bending slopes, and even the passing flocks of your thoughts and your desires.
And to my silence came the laughter of your children in streams, and the longing of your youths in rivers.

This follows no set pattern or codified law, but in the swing and balance of each phrase there is an appeal to the reader's sense of the music of words, just as in the figures and imagery there is a poetic stimulation. Were all so-called free verse of this quality, only the most carping criticism would deny it the name of poetry.

But where, among all the effusions of the modernists, do we find poetry that comes within hailing distance of the glories of *The Prophet* or the lyricism of "The Last Invocation"? Instead, we are asked to acclaim work rhythmically and poetically as deficient as this from T. S. Eliot's *The Waste Land:*

O O O O that Shakespeherian Rag—
It's so elegant
So intelligent
"What shall I do now? What shall I do?"
"I shall rush out as I am, and walk the street
"With my hair down, so. What shall we do tomorrow?
"What shall we ever do?"

We are expected to approve verse as void of singing and poetic qualities as the following, from "The Ordinary Women," by Wallace Stevens:

The lacquered loges huddled there
Mumbled zay-zay and a-zay, a-zay.
The moonlight
Fubbed the girandoles.

Or we are stopped short by lines as encumbered with harsh syllables
as these:

> Over the cleft cliff of her chalk chin.
> —Paul Engle, in *American Child*

>   At once all curves, brow, knee, buttock,
> Flow, flowing in light—*your* light. Brilliant!
> —Hayden Carruth, in *Nothing for Tigers,*
> *Poems 1959–1964*

> Cowhorn-crowned, shockheaded, cornshock-bearded,
> Death is a scarecrow—his death's a teetotum . . .
> —Randall Jarrell, in *The Criterion Book of*
> *American Verse*

> Where X railroad crossing M P 4. 3398 25 W 688
> 4000. 200 496 00 94566 piccaninnies coal trains
> 3 brown pigs tails curled high Poplar Bluffs clang
> 2 scrawny horses 2 clapboard shacks tree bones plains
> Sagging roofs old Fords kids waving outhouses
> Quel est le but social de la poesie Of Thee We Sing
> Bing bong bing bong you're the one for me
> —Daisy Aldan, in *The Destruction of*
> *Cathedrals and Other Poems*

Try to recite any of these selections, try to make it trip from your
tongue, try to put it to music, try to memorize it, and you will
realize how far it departs from all standards that poets in the past
have set for themselves. The best that can be said for these passages
is that they have about the flow of an ice jam. Clogged with close-
packed heavy syllables—curves, brow, knee, buttock, "X railroad
crossing M P 4. 25 W 688," etc.—this work exalts harshness, or at
least makes no attempt to avoid harshness. But one gets the irre-
sistible impression that modern poets do not object to such dis-
sonance; that they are simply not attuned to the delicate pulsations
of sound, even though sound is often the vehicle of sense and though

55

the great poets have driven home their messages by means of chosen and resonant syllables. Of course, if the crows and hawks were to form a singing club, they would deride the notes of the nightingale.

Let me emphasize that, in objecting to the music of the buzz saw, I do not suggest that poets must adhere to a uniformly regular beat —the beat of lines such as

> The curfew tolls the knell of parting day,

or,

> There was a sound of revelry by night,

or, again,

> A hair perhaps divides the false and true.

Such regularity is tolerable throughout extended passages only if offset by graceful variations, as in

> visiting
> This various world with as inconstant wing
> As summer winds that creep from flower to flower,

and,

> O! that this too, too solid flesh would melt,
> Thaw and resolve itself into a dew,

and, once more,

> And there was mounting in hot haste: the steed,
> The mustering squadron and the clattering car,
> Went pouring forward with impetuous speed.

The variations in these passages, while not subject to rule of rote, can be governed only by the sensitive ear attuned to the shades and modulations of sound. To an ear not so attuned, such shades and modulations make no more impression than the subtleties of wit upon a man born without a sense of humor.

3

By way of contrast to the poetry of the new school, read the following:

Morning and evening throughout the various world,
In the procession of the seasons, and in the blue heavens pow-
     dered with stars;
In mountain and plain and many-toned forest;
In the sounding walls of the ocean, and in the billowy seas
     through which we pass in peril from land to land,
We read his thoughts and listen to his voice.
Here do we learn with what far-seeing intelligence he has laid
     the foundations of his everlasting mansion,
How skillfully he has builded its walls, and with what prod-
     igal richness he has decorated all his works.
For the sunlight and the moonlight and the blueness of
     heaven are his;
The sea with its tides; the blackness and the lightnings of the
     tempest,
And snow, and changeful winds, and green and yellow leaf;
His are also the silver rain and the rainbow, the shadows and
     the many-colored mists,
Which he flings like a mantle over the world.

Is the rhythm here not incomparably superior to that of the excerpts from Eliot, Stevens, and the other moderns cited in the preceding pages? Even apart from the imagery, does not the very flow
of the words carry the idea along on a poetic tide? Yet this passage
did not first appear as above. It was contained in the prose of W. H.
Hudson's novel, *A Crystal Age.*

In further illustration of the modern employment of rhythm, consider these examples:

(1)
     The descent beckons
          as the ascent beckoned
               Memory is a kind

of accomplishment
     a sort of renewal
          even
an initiation, since the spaces it opens are new
places
       inhabited by hordes
           heretofore unrealized,
of new kinds—
      since their movements
          are towards new objectives
(even though formerly they were abandoned)

(2)

The first step
     in such clarification
          is to return
     to the original
          meaning
of the word
     as government by
          the people
and to strip it of all other meanings and connotations.

Now which of these passages is meant to have the rhythm of prose, and which the rhythm of poetry? Let me confess that I might have trouble in deciding, had I not extracted the first from the opening piece of William Carlos Williams' *The Desert Music and Other Poems,* whereas the second, which did not originally appear as poetry, was culled quite at random from Walter James Shepherd's disquisition on "Democracy Today" (Bader and Wells, *Essays of Three Decades*).

4

In the attempt to justify jarring and prosy rhythms, the moderns often point to Gerard Manley Hopkins, a minor Victorian generally ignored by his contemporaries despite some work of passing note in the tradition of his day. In his later efforts, we can see the buzz saw in action in tongue-twisting lines. Hopkins was the inventor of the doctrine of "sprung rhythm," which may be illustrated in a passage from "Harry Ploughman":

> Hard as hurdle arms, with a broth of goldish flue,
> Breathed round; the rack of ribs; the scooped flank; lank
> Rope-over thigh; knee-nave; and barrelled shank.

With its clogging heavy feet and its excess of consonants, this moves along with about the ease of rusty wheels on a rocky road. And the same is true of other typical Hopkins work, such as "To What Serves Mortal Beauty?" beginning thus:

> To what serves mortal beauty | —dangerous; does set danc-
> ing blood—the O-seal-that-so | feature, flung prouder form
> Than Purcell tune lets tread to? . . .

Aside from the artificial midline divisions, this is in the mood of much recent writing. And so is this line from "The Leaden Echo and the Golden Echo":

> Winning ways, airs innocent, maiden manners, sweet looks,
> loose locks, long locks, lovelocks, gaygear, going gal-
> lant, girlgrace—

This has exactly the poetic pulse of

> Coffee loose sale, fresh halibut, salmon slices, red yams, dried
> prunes, canned prunes, cream cheese, cured hams, legs
> of mutton, spareribs.

In Hopkins, however, one does not find the further degeneration of rhythm accomplished by many moderns when they deliberately stress unimportant, unaccented syllables. Archibald MacLeish, a frequent offender, has exemplified the method in *Conquistador:*

59

Bleaching with sun and the. . . .

nights in. . . .

elegant knees like the

Girls in Spain and the sand still hot from the sun and the
Surf slow. . . .

wind over. . . .

palm-trees sweeping the

Stars into darkness. . . .

weeks. . . .

waited. . . .

the guns

Brassy in. . . .

loading the cobbed maize and the pigs and

Powder enough for a . . .

ropes on the. . . .

eight tons:

In emphasizing inconsequential words like "the," "a," and "and,"
and so magnifying the trivial and the meaningless, Mr. MacLeish
has gone out of his way to do what poets before his time have carefully avoided. He has made it difficult if not impossible to make the
normal pauses or to read the lines rhythmically, since the eye will
automatically give importance to the last word. It is as if I said to
you, "I will tell you the . . . ," halted for a few seconds, then went
on, "story of a . . . ," then after another few seconds added, "boy I
knew and . . . ," which I followed with another gap, before con-
tinuing, "a girl whom he met in . . ." Such a recitation, of course,
would be maddening. Yet its equivalent in poetry today is regarded
as good form.

Going a step further, we have those purported poems which, by
their printed form, emphasize the hazy nature of the boundary between their rhythms and those of prose. Take this typical passage
from Karl Shapiro's *The Bourgeois Poet:*

New York, killer of poets, do you remember the day you
passed me through your lower intestine? The troop train
paused under Grand Central. That line of women in

mink coats handed us doughnuts through the smutty
windows. They were all crying. For that I forgive New
York. (We smuggled a postcard off at New Haven.)

Perhaps the best comment on these lines is the author's own. At
the top of the page containing the lines, I find the following:

This laisser-aller, this Traumdeutung—am I really a poet?

The inadequacies of such work can best be judged by comparison
with the great rhythmical utterances of earlier poets. We suffer for
lack of lines in which every vowel, every consonant plays its part,
as in

> The moan of doves in immemorial elms,
> And murmuring of innumerable bees,

and

> For the rare and radiant maiden whom the angels name
> Lenore—
> Nameless *here* for evermore.

We need the singing fluency of a Shelley's stanzas on "The Cloud":

> I bring fresh showers for the thirsting flowers,
> From the seas and the streams;
> I bear light shade for the leaves when laid
> In their noonday dreams.

We need the tread of majestic blank verse, as in Wordsworth's
"Tintern Abbey":

> . . . a sense sublime
> Of something far more deeply interfused,
> Whose dwelling is the light of setting suns,
> And the round ocean and the living air,

And the blue sky, and in the mind of man:
A motion and a spirit, that impels
All thinking things, all objects of all thought,
And rolls through all things.

We need music wedded to thought, as in Arthur O'Shaughnessy's often-quoted "Ode":

We are the music-makers,
   And we are the dreamers of dreams,
Wandering by lone sea-breakers,
   And sitting by desolate streams.

And we need free, original, and yet controlled use of rhythm, as in Robert Bridges' "A Passer-By":

Whither, O splendid ship, thy white sails crowding,
   Leaning across the bosom of the urgent West,
That fearest nor sea rising, nor sky clouding,
   Whither away, fair rover, and what thy quest?

Not all these poems may accord with the modern style in theme or spirit. But their rhythms are expressions of the everlasting nature of poetry. And so long as such rhythms are ignored, poetry will limp, grope, and stumble if it does not entirely cease to be.

V

THE CHILL OF
THE KNIFE-EDGE

I

If your best friend were to tell you that he was in love, you would be unlikely to reply, "You are experiencing a biological equation, transmitted by ancestral intermediaries." If an acquaintance were to confide that his mother had died, the last thing you would think of saying would be, "Well, I hope the old girl enjoyed the merry performance." And if you had just attended your grandfather's funeral, you would consider it inappropriate to remark, "7 x 7, plus 4 x 6 —more years than there are squares on a checkerboard—death cashiered in the old guy, after a life spent in squabbling, cheating, racketeering." So far as I know, no one has ever made these precise statements; yet someone might very well have made them in modern poems, for they are in the modern mood of detachment, of aloofness, of objectivity, of an emotional frigidity that chills like a knife-edge.

This tendency is by no means the product of a day or of a year; it can be traced back fifty years or more. Amy Lowell, the high priestess of the new movement in the second decade of this century, writes thus of love in her poem "A Gift":

> See! I give myself to you, Beloved!
> My words are little jars

For you to take and put upon a shelf.
Their shapes are quaint and beautiful . . .

When I shall have given you the last one
You will have the whole of me,
But I shall be dead.

Here, if ever there was one, is a cerebral love poem. You may be
certain that, if any woman in actual life ever spoke thus to her be-
loved, she left him mute and frozen.

Even more pallid and chilly, to my way of thinking, are these
lines on "Death" by Maxwell Bodenheim, a poet of some promi-
nence in the nineteen-twenties:

I shall walk down the road.
I shall turn and feel upon my feet
The kisses of Death, like scented rain.
For Death is a black slave with little silver birds
Perched in a sleeping wreath upon his head.
He will tell me, his voice like jewels
Dropped into a satin bag,
How he has tip-toed after me down the road . . .

Is this the way that any human being has actually felt about the
solemn, mysterious transformation that awaits us all? Is this the
feeling of the poet as he contemplates his own end? Does he really
imagine that death will come to him as "a black slave with little
silver birds perched in a sleeping wreath upon his head"? Or has
Bodenheim approached his theme without emotion, deliberately
suppressing his natural feelings in favor of cold fancies? If so, what
meaning can such fancies have for the man or woman face to face
with the most portentous of experiences?

But Amy Lowell, Maxwell Bodenheim, and their colleagues
would matter not at all today if they had not set the pattern that is
still followed—followed, however, with greater eccentricities of
expression. Suppose that we turn to some lines from T. S. Eliot's
"Burnt Norton":

Garlic and sapphires in the mud
Clot the bedded axle-tree.
The trilling wire in the blood
Sings below inveterate scars
And reconciles forgotten wars.

This is not extreme. It is merely typical of the impersonal aloofness of the modern. Characteristically, it radiates no warmth.
No warmth, likewise, is released by Robert Lowell's "The Death
of the Sheriff":

>   . . . Soon
> The undertaker who collects antiques
> Will let his motor idle at the door
> And set his pine-box on the parlor floor.
> Our homicidal sheriff howled for weeks;
> We kiss. The State had reasons: on the whole,
> It acted out of kindness when it locked
> Its servant in this place and had him watched,
> Until an ordered darkness left his soul
> A *tabula rasa;* when the Angel knocked
> The sheriff laid his notched
> Revolver on the table for the guest.

In a briefer passage, Robert Lowell gives us the following:

> In the grandiloquent lettering on Mother's coffin,
> *Lowell* had been misspelled *LOVEL.*
> The corpse
> was wrapped like *panetone* in Italian tinfoil.

One asks how any man, swept by the emotion of his mother's
death, could think such details worth noting. But, of course, the
author's idea is to convey no feeling except of shock.
In this he is somewhat in the mood of John Ciardi speaking of the
passing of his father:

It took four flowerboats to convey my father's black
Cadillac cruiser out to St. Mike's and down
deeper than all salt. It was a very successful
funeral my mother remembers remembering.

A less irreverent but hardly less frigid manifestation of the knife-
edge may be seen in Winfred Townley Scott's "Mr. Whittier":

In any case, here is a city, founded in 1630, present population
        somewhere about
55,000—has been more in boom times, and has been a lot less;
        —say
In three hundred years has birthed a couple of hundred thou-
        sand people
And one poet. Not bad. . . .

To me this carries about the poetic impact of a census report. It
conveys no emotional or imaginative impression, no suggestion of
the appearance of the city or of its thousands of inhabitants, no idea
of what any of them are like inside. The thoughts, hopes, longings,
passions of not one of all those multitudes are made plain—not the
tears of a single mother for a lost son, the cries of a single child for
a missing playmate, the laughter of a single youth, the desires,
struggles, ambitions, sorrows, and secret heroism of any of that
motley host. Yet of such things poetry is made. Poetry has no relationship whatever to cold, objective, statistical computations of
population.

Nor is poetry, as I see it, to be found in a description such as this
from Horace Gregory's "Suburban Hostel: Hudson River View," in
Medusa in Gramercy Park:

Up where The Nursing Home unfolds its whiteness,
A starched girl drives a wheel chair with one hand,
Consults her watch and slowly reads a chart:
"Patient 15 believes his room a cell,
His bed a grave, sets fire to his mattress,

Will not play golf or bridge, refuses hobbies,
Nor paints, nor draws, nor hopes to drive a car,
Simulates deafness, talks of 'inner life,'
A stubborn case who smiles and never weeps,
Seems happy, yet remote—a sign of danger."
The girl rereads her watch, yawns, sighs, lights up
A cigarette—

Here there is nothing freakish or eccentric, and the blank verse follows an acceptable rhythm. But here is a better-than-average example of the modern objective method, which results in no responsive throb in the reader, no warmth of insight or of fellow feeling. Contrast this with the subjective report in Pauline Avery Crawford's *Sonnets from a Hospital:*

Shut doors along the hall like sleeping eyes,
Veiling their shadowy secrets I could see;
Nor what dim shapes they sheltered could surmise,
What spirits spent, or in what agony;
Nor through the clouded hours could understand
Why entering angels graciously forebore,
As if restrained by an omniscient hand,
To shut me off—to close my open door.
Of angels what archangel's listening ears,
Attuned to what strange silences of woe,
Hearing the dropping of what phantom tears
From eyelids ever tearless, thus could know
How very long in darkness I had been
Behind a door no one could enter in?

Here one shares in the author's experience and penetrates with her to the vibrant depths in which all poetry is born.

When a writer feels as this writer manifestly feels her confinement in the hospital, he will express himself in the simplest, most direct way. He will not allow his work to be burdened by theories; he will not strike a pose nor try to seem "new" or "different"; he will head straight toward his goal, saying just what he has to say.

If, for example, he recalls the death of one dear to him, he might begin with something as plain and unassuming as:

> Ten years ago my sister died;
>   The clouds hung low and gray;
> And brooding where the grim gulls glide
> Dully I watched the ebbing tide
>   Half of the desolate day.

While this is not outstanding poetry, it might transmit a real emotion to the reader. But suppose that the emotion is not genuine. Suppose that the author has no thoughts or feelings concerning his sister, and nevertheless wishes to impress others with a poem. He might then begin in this way:

> Ten years ago
> in the alternating cycles of human existence
> that aggregation of protoplasmic substance
> known as my sister
> (her name was Ann, but what is a name to
>   a graveworm?)
> suffered a sharp chemical disintegration
> and left me with a protracted sorrow . . .

One thing we may be sure of: the author's sorrow could not have been too protracted. Nor had he really anything to say about the death of his sister: a man who did have something to say would not be troubled about a "protoplasmic substance" or "a sharp chemical disintegration."

This example, to be sure, may seem extreme, and does indeed verge toward the comical, though hardly more so than many seriously intended modern poems that glitter with a cold fire. We have already noted several, and others are not far to seek. Take this couplet from George Barker's "Sacred Elegy: Separation of Man from God":

> Everyone walking everywhere goes in a glow
> Of geometrical progression, all meteors in praise . . .

Or witness this from Kenneth Rexroth's "The Signature of All Things":

> We have escaped the bitterness
> Of love, and love lost, and love
> Betrayed. And what might have been,
> And what might be, fall equally
> Away with what is, and leave
> Only those ideograms
> Printed on the immortal
> Hydrocarbons of flesh and stone.

Or glance at these lines from Edith Sitwell's "The April Rain," which is supposed to represent the speech of boy to girl:

> The sapphire dews sing like a star; bird-breasted dew
> Lies like a bird and flies
>
> In the singing wood and is blown by the bright air
> Upon your wood-wild April-soft long hair
> That seems the rising of spring constellations—
> Aldebaran, Procyon, Sirius,
> And Cygnus who gave you all his bright swan-plumage.

It is safe to assume that no boy ever addressed a girl in this way. It is equally safe to assume that if a boy did try to address a girl in this way, the affair would make little progress. The cold glitter of "Aldebaran, Procyon, Sirius, and Cygnus" (the first three of which, incidentally, are not constellations) can have no reference whatever to the warmth of human emotion; they are as much in place in a love poem as icicles would be in a bridal gown. There is no reason to suppose that Miss Sitwell, like some of the other poets quoted, deliberately strove to strike with a chilly blade. But it is evident that she set out to write a poem of the emotions without having the emotional equipment of poetry. It should surprise no one if the results verge upon the ridiculous.

As far back as our records go, poetry has been a thing of tears and laughter, the expression of man's vaulting heights and of his crying depths, of his agonies and ecstasies, his rage and fear and wonder. Even though tempered by the mind, always the heart and not the cerebrum has ruled and has made poetry possible. This is notably true in Homer, in both *The Iliad* and *The Odyssey*. Take the meeting of Odysseus with his mother's shade (Book XI, translated by J. W. Mackail):

> So said she: but I inly for a space
> Mused and was full of longing to embrace
> The soul of my dead mother. Thrice I sprang
> Toward her, fain to clasp her face to face;
>
> And thrice from out my hands to clasp her spread
> Like to a shadow or a dream she fled.
> And grief waxed ever keener at my heart . . .

Here one can tremble at the hero's tense emotion, as at the passion of the dead Agamemnon when he encounters Odysseus:

> Straightway he knew me and let fall a flood
> Of tears, and shrilly weeping, stretched his hands
> Toward me, fain to clasp me where I stood.

It is safe to say that an enduring source of the popularity of both Homeric epics is the pulsating emotion, which gives the work a human reality and an appeal that persist amid all the changes in man's social condition. And the same is true of other early poetry, such as the Scottish and English ballads, which, for all their economy of expression, vibrate with feeling:

> I wish I were where Helen lies,
> Night and day on me she cries;
> O that I were where Helen lies
> On fair Kirconnell lea!

The same, also, is true of Shakespeare throughout the gigantic panorama of his characters, as in the pathetic exclamation of King Lear upon the death of his daughter Cordelia:

> Howl, howl, howl, howl. O, you are men of stone:
> Had I your tongues and eyes, I'ld use them so
> That heaven's vault should crack. She's gone for ever! . . .
> She's dead as earth.

In the reiterated "She's gone for ever!" as in the ensuing passionate outburst, "Why should a dog, a horse, a rat, have life,/And thou no breath at all?" Lear speaks not only for himself but for millions throughout the centuries. And he speaks in poetry that mere coldness, mere objectivity could not have created.

Milton, even amid the Olympian grandeurs of *Paradise Lost,* does not disdain emotion, of which he makes effective use when Satan hurls his resolute defiance of the Almighty:

> Farewell happy fields,
> Where Joy for ever dwells! Hail horrours! hail
> Infernal world! and thou, profoundest Hell,
> Receive thy new possessor: one who brings
> A mind not to be changed by place or time.
> The mind is its own place, and in itself
> Can make a Heav'n of Hell, a Hell of Heav'n.
> What matter where, if I be still the same . . .
> Better to reign in Hell than serve in Heav'n!

Wordsworth can be emotional not only in the Lucy poems and other simple lyrics but in a sonnet such as the one beginning:

> Surprised by joy—impatient as the Wind,
> I turned to share the transport—O! with whom
> But Thee, deep buried in the silent tomb,
> That spot which no vicissitude can find?

Tennyson, with "emotion recollected in tranquillity," has injected a melancholy splendor into his great elegy *In Memoriam,* in which the reader cannot help sharing the poet's feeling:

Dark house, by which once more I stand
  Here in the long unlovely street,
  Doors, where my heart was used to beat
So quickly, waiting for a hand,

A hand that can be clasped no more—
  Behold me, for I cannot sleep,
  And like a guilty thing I creep
At earliest morning to the door.

He is not here; but far away
  The noise of life begins again,
  And ghastly thro' the drizzling rain
On the bald street breaks the blank day.

The early Yeats could touch the heart with a singing emotion:

When you are old and grey and full of sleep,
And nodding by the fire, take down this book,
And slowly read, and dream of the soft look
Your eyes had once, and of their shadows deep . . .

A restrained emotion radiates from the lines of Masefield:

Be with me, Beauty, for the fire is dying,
My dog and I are old, too old for roving.

Emotion to which most of us will respond animates Vachel Lindsay's "Abraham Lincoln Walks at Midnight":

It is portentous, and a thing of state
That here at midnight, in our little town,
A mourning figure walks, and will not rest,
Near the old court-house pacing up and down.

And emotion transfuses the more than hundred pages of one of the moving long poems of our century, William Ellery Leonard's sonnet-narrative of a tragic love, *Two Lives,* whose pathos is evident in the refrain of the concluding section:

(O Earth-and-Autumn of the Setting Sun,
She is not by, to know my task is done!)

3

You will note that all these examples are from poems first published decades ago. I cite no recent poems for the reason that contemporary poems of the emotions are difficult to discover. Why should this be? Chiefly because of the attitudes of our times, the skepticism and the scientific and philosophical materialism, which have been reflected in critical judgments and poetic moods. Somewhat like the Stoic philosophers of old, who distrusted emotion and therefore clung to a creed of iron, we treat the tender and feeling part of man as something weak and unworthy if not nonexistent. The Stoics generally speaking, however, were not creative artists.

It is characteristic of our outlook that we make little distinction between sentiment and sentimentality. Yet the first expresses that undercurrent of true feeling without which life would be cold, dull, and flat as a stone floor, while the second is the mere disease of sentiment—its unhealthy excess, its dishonest imitation and exaggeration. Whereas true sentiment may speak in lines as plain and simple as Thomas Hood's

> For when the morn came dim and sad,
>   And chill with early showers,
> Her quiet eyelids closed—she had
>   Another morn than ours

—sentimentality may rant and gesticulate, with an excess of emphasis, as in this by Vilate Primrose Dodson, in Katie May Gill's anthology, *Mother:*

> I love every scrap in that Calico Quilt
> For it was made by my Mother;
> I love every stitch in that Calico Quilt
> They were stitched by my Mother.
> There's a piece of Sister's dress;
> There's a scrap from Brother's . .

This, which is no worse than many that might be cited, may be meant to impress. But it gives the effect of extravagance rather than of genuine emotion. In objecting to work of this type, the moderns (and not only the moderns) are thoroughly justified. Unfortunately, what the innovators do is to throw out the baby along with the baby clothes; and they do not even appear to try to distinguish between the two.

In life's ordinary relationships, sentiment is rarely absent. If you chance upon a friend in a bus, if you welcome guests to your home, if you celebrate a wedding or an anniversary or reminisce over a long-past meeting, if you learn of a birth or a death or of honors newly bestowed upon an acquaintance, you will feel some sort of sentiment unless you are colder at heart than an octopus. Why then should sentiment, at least on its higher levels, not be reflected in poetry?

But here we come face to face with the modern creed of objectivity. The poet, we are told, should look upon human affairs with a dispassionate gaze, as from above. Yet we fail to reflect that this, in effect, is to say that he should no longer be a poet, for the poet, of all men, is most concerned with what occurs in the depths of his fellow beings, with the struggles and agonies and triumphs of the inner self. To be entirely objective, we would require the attitude of an automaton appraising an automaton. One hundred percent objectivity, in other words, is impossible; we all look out upon the world with the eyes of our subjective beings, and we can look upon it in no other way. Even the statistician cannot be wholly objective, since he weighs and interprets his figures by means of his mind. Even the mathematician, when he applies the results of his researches, departs from absolute objectivity. If the moderns went all the way toward their goal of truly objective poems, they could not stop short of work such as this:

$$xya - 14yz^2 - (py)^{-4} - \frac{p}{q} = \sqrt[3]{\frac{o}{0}}$$
$$x - y - z = o^n$$

This, in effect, is what many moderns have given us. The excerpts that follow are not, to my mind, greatly preferable as poetry to algebraic equations:

K E I	M E N	RAN	K E I
K I U	M A N	MAN	K E I
JITSU	GETSU	K O	KWA
T A N	FUKU	TAN	K A I

—Ezra Pound, in "Canto XLIX"

Soutine trumpet
Derain eel
Seurat hourglass
Pissarro dhow
Rousseau corolla
Bonheur conch
Rubens narwhal
Velasquez groin

—May Swenson (recipient of a Rockefeller grant and of the Robert Frost Fellowship in Poetry in 1957), in *A Cage of Spines*

Lat quis? cf. Engl. he him it (for older hit)

POS (Pronoun)

but quantus is posos

v. sub. pos

so Skt

p of Ionian Grk is k

kati = s quantus

kas, ka = quis, quae
kva = qua
kutus = quo
katha = qui   quomodo
kada = quum

kataras = poteros, uter

—Charles Olson, in *Proprioception*

75

THE FIRE

jump	stone	hand	leaf	shadow	sun
day	plash	coin	light	downstream	fish
first	loosen	under	boat	harbor	circle
old	earth	bronze	dark	wall	waver
new	smell	purl	close	wet	green
now	rise	foot	warm	hold	cool

—Robert Duncan, in *Poetry*

setendresse tendressetendresse tendressete
nderdresstenderdresstenderdresstenderdre
ssetendresse tendressetendresse tendresset
enderdresstenderdresstenderdresstenderdr
essetendressetendresse tendressetendresse
—Ian Hamilton Finlay, in *Pogammoggan,* No. I

Are further examples necessary? These passages, in any case, will serve as an introduction to the subject matter of the next chapter.

VI

CLARITY IS NO CRIME

I

No reader has ever had to ponder the meaning of the familiar old nursery rhyme beginning:

> Mary had a little lamb,
> Its fleece was white as snow,
> And everywhere that Mary went
> The lamb was sure to go.

This, to be sure, is not exalted poetry. But it does say what it has to say, and it is clear and simple. It would not have been improved had the author expressed his thoughts as follows:

> The female member of the *genus homo*
> Designated conventionally by the nomenclature of Mary
> Had proprietory rights
> Over an iceberg-white infantile wool-bearing ruminant
> Which matched its perambulations to her own.

This sounds forced and murky as well as ridiculous. Yet this is in the style of many modern poems, and illustrates how some verse writers will go out of their way to make simple things appear complex.

Let us go on to other examples. A man wishing to inform a neighbor that his house is on fire would not rush to him with the cry that "An oxygen-hydrocarbon reaction, with a vast heat-releasing potential, is threatening drastic molecular rearrangements in your domicile!" A youth who wanted to announce that he had graduated from college would not state, "The academic pinnacles and ridges, classified in graduated species of knowledge and betokened by appellations from A to D, have been officially surmounted." And a girl desiring to inform you of her engagement would not report that "Biological suasions, genetic, ancestral, and racial, furthered by my individual idiosyncrasies, are propelling me toward a socially sanctioned compact with a masculine partner."

But all this, you will say, is absurd. No one—at least, no sane person—ever spoke with such preposterous pomposity. Granted! Yet this is just how some of our poets do speak. We have seen some examples, and, unfortunately, there is no scarcity of others. Read, for instance, these lines from Theodore Roethke's "The Shape of the Fire":

> Last night I slept in the pits of a tongue.
> The silver fish ran in and out of my special bindings;
> I grew tired of the ritual of names and the assistant keeper of
>   the molluscs:
> Up over a viaduct I came, to the snakes and sticks of another
>   winter,
> A two-legged dog hunting a new horizon of howls.

Try to fathom this, from "Syndrome: Extra Visitors," by Kenneth H. Ford, in the poetry magazine *WW*:

> Time? When are we leaving here?
> Tree-hung bird obstreperous said.
> Backwards the bomb falls heavy
> for in the inosculate womb of war worlds
> many pretties compete for the mommy-flavor;
>
> still
> cardiac-terror breaks its syndrome

against these harder city grains,
plush seats suspended during offal hours. . . .

Or puzzle out this on the subject of "The Poets' Annual Indigence Report," from William Stafford's book, *Traveling Through the Dark*:

Tonight beyond the determined moon,
aloft with nothing left that is voluntary
for delight, everything uttering hydrogen,
your thinkers are mincing along through a hail of contingen-
cies . . .

Again, try to absorb these lines, from "Hymn to Reductive Thought" in a recent paperback by Frederick Bock:

There's
No ever-after fallen at His nameless feet,
But when I pick it up and see
If only the fountain running in the breeze,

Tense and pretense together (though the *ligne donnée*
Swings in my art but the shadow of a heart)
    Still unmask
A brillianter kind of vanishing-point
    than zero.

A modern device so common as to have become almost hackneyed is that of spreading confusion by omitting punctuation, as in "Chant for All the People on Earth," by Leslie Woolf Hedley, in Walter Lowenfels' anthology, *Poets of Today*:

Not to forget not to ever forget so long as you live so long as you love so long as you breathe eat wash walk think see feel read touch laugh not to forget not to ever forget so long as you know the meaning of freedom of what lonely nights are to torn lovers so long as you retain the soul heart of a man . . .

Even the poets of classical antiquity are reduced by the moderns to jumbles of meaningless incoherence. Consider the following, from "Versions of Catullus," by Celia and Louis Zukofsky in *Poetry*:

> Out nil little pallor cue in time conceding her, deigned your
> looks, my ah say knows true, came to light agreed my own,
> when circumstance coursing all link sigh paid Cupid o
> full gay bout crocus now candid use in tunica.

Whatever you may think of such an exercise in obscurity, how do you explain the next example? Contributed by Douglas Blazek to *The Poetry Review* of the University of Tampa, it opens thus:

a girl with

sandals
for EyEs

dri
nk
i
n
g   the t*e*a of moon

EE
with bric-a-brac for   t   th

F
E
L   field
L   into a   poppy/death

&   f o r e v e r

2

But let us return to work that has at least the semblance of sanity. "A Is for Alpha: Alpha Is for A," by Conrad Aiken, is less difficult to interpret than some of the preceding selections, though here again the author goes out of his way to spread a screen between himself and his readers:

Now it begins. Now the subaqueous evening
exemplary as the inalterable moon
begins again to begin. With slight starts
of organ-grinder music (if the scene
is of city) or of '*dee-dee-dee*—!'
chickadee trill if (as it is) it is country.

If Mr. Aiken had said what he intended to say more simply,
directly, and clearly, would he have been less poetic? Did another
American poet of this century, Ridgely Torrence, forsake the canons
of poetry by his clarity in these first two stanzas of "Santa Barbara
Beach"?

> Now while the sunset offers,
>   Shall we not take our own:
> The gems, the blazing coffers,
>   The seas, the shores, the throne?
>
> The sky-ships, radiant-masted
>   Move out, bear low our way.
> Oh, Life was dark while it lasted,
>   Now for enduring day.

This, to my mind, is the more poetic because of its simplicity and
clarity. It is hard to see how, without these qualities, it could convey its poetic message.

True, it would be dangerous to rely exclusively upon simplicity
and clarity, for while sometimes of great help to the poet and his
audience, they do not of themselves create poetry; otherwise, the
news columns of our daily papers would be contributions to the
Muse. But this self-evident truth seems to have been forgotten by
many modernists. Only so can we account for lines such as Kenneth
Rexroth's

> I didn't want it, you wanted it,
> Now you've got it and you don't like it.
> You can't get out of it now,

or Kenneth Fearing's

Enter the proprietor of the Riviera Cafe;
Remarks, "It is a wonderful morning," as in fact it always is,
    for him . . .

These passages leave nothing to be desired in the way of clarity.
Yet they leave everything to be desired in the way of poetry. How
can this be? A basic fact, which appears to have been generally
ignored of late, is that poetry can be created neither by clarity alone
nor by its opposite. Poetry springs from some inner quality that may
be aided but cannot be produced by clarity; poetry may be hard to
fathom or as transparent as spring water—but no poetry was ever
helped by obscurity, and least of all by obscurity deliberately introduced. On the contrary, much of the world's great poetry has appeal
chiefly because it is clear. For this reason, and because communication is literature's very reason for being, every poet who has valued
his art above mere posing has tried to make his work as clear as his
subject matter has permitted. Not all have succeeded; but this may
be attributed largely to the difficulties of their themes, while sometimes (in the case of poets of past generations) the failure may be
ascribed to changes in language and in social outlook or even to new
educational methods and approaches.

3

Certain poets and critics nowadays not only practice obscurity;
they preach it, reminding one of the old grandame who holds that
the bitterer the medicine the better for the patient. The view seems
to be that, in order really to benefit from poetry, one should labor
and groan and suffer in the dark. This attitude was illustrated some
time ago in a poetry magazine:

Real poetry is more often than not hard to read. Not much
of it can be read rapidly, or quite understood at a first reading. . . . It is condensed, figurative, symbolic, implicative expression.

The author does not say that if verse is not hard to read it is not poetry, but one cannot help gathering this impression. The chief error of this writer and of his group, of course, is in their assumption that poetry is written for and by a limited number of aesthetes, who communicate with one another by secret code and dwell in some blue empyrean high above the base, uncomprehending masses.

A more determined defense of obscurity occurs in a book by the noted British critic Herbert Read, *The Nature of Literature*. On behalf of the obscure poem, he makes this incredible statement: "That Shakespeare is an obscure poet is witnessed . . . by the immense libraries of elucidatory criticism which have been devoted to his text." With an astonishing disregard of literary history, the author ignores the fact that great volumes of "elucidatory criticism" have been devoted to every pre-eminent writer, whether obscure or not. He fails to note the obscurities introduced in Shakespeare by changes in language and custom for which the poet was in no way responsible. And he overlooks the confusions, not injected by the bard himself, which have been added by critical disputations and interpretations, as well as by the uncertainties as to text and authorship.

On even more dubious grounds, Mr. Read maintains that obscurity is a "positive value":

> . . . there is a fundamental obscurity in the actual thought process involved—an obscurity due to the honesty and objectivity of the poet. He works outwards from an emotional unity. This unity may be clothed in what Vossler calls "an inner language form"; but between this inner language form and the outer language form in which our everyday rational thoughts are expressed, there is no necessary correspondence. In order to remain faithful to the inner language form, the poet must invent words and create images, he must mishandle and stretch the meaning of words.

Here is attempted justification for the modern versifiers who do indeed "mishandle and stretch the meaning of words." But the critic does not show us how "honesty and objectivity" can produce obscurity: if correct, he has given us a powerful argument for dishonesty. Furthermore, Mr. Read does not make it clear what he means by "an inner language form." But, of course, it might be inconsistent to defend poetic obscurity in lucid prose.

4

Literature is not the only field deliberately thrown into confusion by muddied or black lenses. We are familiar with the politician concealing his plans or his lack of plans and ideas behind spouts of words in which all is as clear as a marsh fog. Likewise, we realize that many religions have practiced obscurity in order to confuse or mystify the credulous. The witch doctor, beating his tom-tom and mumbling his weird-sounding incantations, is but one example, an example in the same spirit as the modern poet scribbling unintelligible gabble. Both are but following a common human tendency to shed darkness so as to impress; the unknown often seems superior to the known. No one can say what treasures the murky pond may not conceal.

But not all obscurity in poetry is intentional. Much of it undoubtedly occurs because the poet has not mastered his medium or is unwilling to exert himself to wipe away opaque patches. But I would go further and say that a major part of the current obscurity reflects the clouds in the poet's mind. Suppose, for example, that he would like to write a philosophical poem, regardless of whether he has any philosophical ideas. He has, in any case, a passing acquaintance with some common philosophical terms, and hopes to use these to say something impressive. His chief need, of course, is to give the appearance of profundity, of penetrating insights which he need not explain—the perceptive reader will grasp them without the childish necessity of being told what they are all about. Hence the writer, after prodding his brain cells, begins as follows:

Time . . . circumstance . . . destiny
Multiplicity of congruents

Concurrent, successive, substantive, retroactive,
The howl of the dog, the gasp of the hawk's victim, the yelp
    of the wildcat,
Man inverted and man involuted,
Postulates, vicissitudes, concepts, indirections, uncertainties,
Cradles, bridal wreaths, grave-sheets,
Time . . . circumstance . . . destiny.

Now certainly this, whatever its poetic qualities, sounds as if it ought to mean something. I might go so far as to say that it could even be interpreted to mean something—that is, if the reader is willing to twist his eyes almost out of focus. Not that what it says would be worth saying; it would amount at best to platitudes ponderously piled up. Nevertheless, many readers, not wishing to admit their ignorance or incomprehension, might declare themselves to be impressed. Many might really be impressed, feeling that there must be profound meaning here, all the profounder because they could not understand it. In fact, the author himself might be impressed, particularly if his offering came to be widely praised. He might flatter himself that he had said something notable, even if he was not sure just what he had said or exactly what about it was notable.

Innumerable modern poems, including some of those already cited, give evidence of having been written in this way. Take, as another example, Theodore Weiss' geometrically arranged "A Local Matter," in his book *Outlanders:*

> till I, skinned,
> glistening, one of many
> hides racked in a row, lesser
> tale in a larger, from the lean-
> to of noon, sink to mouse, catgut,
> fiddlings of some nameless bog.

Or read this, by Harold Norse, in *The Dancing Beasts:*

> Failure is no loss—it's the flag of Good
> humility's stemma on the wood of blood

where time must yield
whiteness of bones before the white light
of the painless infinite.

Or glance at these lines by Chris Bjerknes on "Humpbacked Dolphins" in the little magazine *Experiment:*

OUT of the dead sea, Adam
    and the tides
through the inland eye where the gulls
    like vultures taunt the hair of the circular
dream

      the sea more
        ferryman fish regresser from
      the sea-weed
walls and gestalt gulfs and sharks
    devouring
      to regret the sun's rising
the shallow shadows bleed
and stars pulsed by drums of sleep

      regret and spineless nettles and whose
    a freud
strand animus, and simple spawning power.

Can you believe that the author has something to say, and has set out with a firm intention to say it?

It may be, of course, that Mr. Bjerknes did have some idea of what he meant by gulls that "taunt the hair of the circular dream," "shallow shadows" that "bleed," and "stars pulsed by drums of sleep." Unfortunately, he has neglected to share this knowledge with the reader.

But after all, can one really blame the unknown aspirant for resorting to concealment rather than to communication when he is following the model flaunted before him by the praised and prize-winning supposedly great writer? What shall one expect of the novice when the acclaimed master T. S. Eliot can give us the following in his renowned *The Waste Land:*

London Bridge is falling down falling down falling down
Poi s'ascose nel foco che gli affina
Quando fiam uti chelidon—O swallow swallow
Le Prince d'Aquitaine à la tour abolie
These fragments I have shored against my ruins
Why then Ile fit you. Hieronymo's mad againe.
Datta. Dayadhvam. Damyata.
           Shantih   shantih   shantih

No matter if the name of great Shakespeare were signed to this, I would say that it was mere affected drivel, mere playacting unrelated to poetry, obscure gibberish meant to impress but not to communicate. And regarding a passage such as this from Canto LXXVII, by Ezra Pound, I should say exactly the same:

"the mind of Plato . . . or that of Bacon"   said Upward
        seeking parallel for his own
"Haff you gno bolidigal basshunts? . . . .
Demokritoos, Heragleitos" exclaimed Doktor Slonimsky 1912

So Miscio sat in the dark lacking the gasometer penny
    but then said: "Do you speak German?"

    to Asquith, in 1914

"How Ainley face work all the time
                back of that mask"
But Mrs Tinkey never believed he wanted her cat
for mouse-chasing
          and not for oriental cuisine

If such disconnected ramblings convey any poetic impression, then we have missed some important poetry by not recording the vaporings of the lunatics in our asylums.

VII

HAVE WE FORGOTTEN IMAGINATION?

Two men, whom we may call Bob and Bert, were walking together in a wood. "What do you see here?" asked Bob.

"Why, some trees, of course," answered Bert. "Also, a path, some rotting logs, and some old decaying stumps."

"And is that all?"

"What else is there? What do you see, Bob?"

"Well," replied Bob, indicating a tangle of foliage, "I see two pythons looped around each other. I see a crouching tiger ready to spring, and an antlered deer taking fright and about to flee. Over there, in what you may take to be a thick clump of young trees, I see two lovers embracing, and an angel bending over them with a harp. Down beneath, crocodiles are crawling in the mud toward an animal like a four-horned horse. I see a Medusa with hair like green sea-grass, and a Gorgon—"

"But that's imagination—mere imagination!" Bert interrupted, impatiently. And, obviously, he was right. However, the conversation had illustrated the difference between the matter-of-fact observer who sees only what his senses show him, and the imaginative man who creates his own universes. The former, throughout the ages, has been the practical, nonartistic man. But the ranks of the latter, at least until our own day, have included most of our artists and all of our poets.

The matter-of-fact man—to bring out some further differences between the two types—might have said in regard to a certain historic situation, "How happy York has made me!" But Shakespeare, the man of imagination, wrote:

> Now is the winter of our discontent
> Made glorious summer by this sun of York.

The matter-of-fact man, gazing at the skies, might have remarked, "How misty the moon is tonight!" But the poet Shelley saw through different eyes:

> And, like a dying lady lean and pale,
> Who totters forth, wrapp'd in a gauzy veil,
> Out of her chamber, led by the insane
> And feeble wanderings of her fading brain,
> The moon arose up in the murky east,
> A white and shapeless mass.

The matter-of-fact man, noting the evanescence of life, might have lamented, "Too bad that youth ends so soon!" But the poet Omar Khayyam, as interpreted by Edward Fitzgerald, reflected:

> Yet Ah, that Spring should vanish with the Rose!
> That Youth's sweet-scented manuscript should close!
> The Nightingale that in the branches sang,
> Ah whence, and whither flown again, who knows!

These are but examples, of which thousands could be cited. The poet in all cases, by using his imagination and the images supplied by his imagination, has been able to soar to heights that the unimaginative plodder could no more approach than the mole could fly to the eagle's eyrie. Only through the imagination did poetry originally become possible; and imagination has always sustained and conveyed its messages.

In our own period, however, a great change has occurred. Along with rhythm and emotional content and other qualities formerly deemed essential, imagination has been dethroned. Byron, were he alive today, would not be applauded for finding that

> The mind can make
> Substance, and people planets of its own
> With beings brighter than have been, and give
> A breath to forms which can outlive all flesh.

Shakespeare, if referring to our own world, could not include the poet in his listing:

> The lunatic, the lover, and the poet
> Are of imagination all compact.

Nor could he state that

> . . . as imagination bodies forth
> The forms of things unknown, the poet's pen
> Turns them to shapes, and gives to airy nothing
> A local habitation and a name.

The fact is that the approved poets today refer not to "the forms of things unknown" but to the shapes of things known; "airy nothing" is to them of no consequence beside concrete something, such as shirts, socks, and potatoes. Consider these lines by Adrien Stoutenburg on the theme of the tragic South Polar expedition of Captain Robert F. Scott and four companions—a subject brimming with immense possibilities for resounding and imaginative epic poetry:

> Sunday, February 26:
> Minus seventeen. Rations short, fuel shorter.
> *We want more food* . . . Yet, Evans had helped a bit by
> dying.
> A march of six and one half miles at morning.
> Nine hours more; add eleven miles.
> *I wish we could have some help from the wind.*
> Forty-three miles to the next depot.

Monday:
 Minus thirty-seven. *Desperately cold.*
 Land disappearing in a satisfactory manner.
 We may find ourselves in safety at the next depot,
 but there is a horrid element of doubt.

In this dull, totally undistinguished prose there is no question of "The poet's eye, in a fine frenzy rolling."

On the same level is the work of John Berryman, which has recently enjoyed considerable vogue. His book, *77 Dream Songs,* has all the imaginative fervor of a cash register:

> Henry sats in de bar & was odd,
> off in the glass from the glass,
> at odds wif de world & its god,
> his wife is a complete nothing, . . .

> Old Pussy-cat if he won't eat, he don't
> feel good in his tum', old Pussy-cat.
> He *wants* to have eaten. . . .

Acacia, burnt myrrh, velvet, pricky stings.
—I'm not so young but not so very old,
said screwed-up lovely 23.
A final sense of being right out in the cold,
unkissed.
(—My psychiatrist can lick your psychiatrist.) Women get
 under things.

These are but typical passages. Could anything be further from the mood of poetry? Compare Berryman's lines with Keats' often quoted

> magic casements, opening on the foam
> Of perilous seas, in faery lands forlorn.

Contrast the spirit of Berryman with that of one of the most distinguished of twentieth-century poets, John Masefield, who in a production of his old age, *Old Raiger and Other Verse,* can give us lines like these:

> At this, her radiant beauty grew so bright,
> The towers, with their pyramids, so glowed,
> I could no longer see them for the light:
> Light, and more light, through which no image showed;
> The light that ended chaos, light that saves,
> That brings the Spring and triumphs over graves.

You cannot conceive of this passage without imagination, just as you cannot picture John Berryman writing in his present style if he used as much imagination as the plainest of the Mother Goose rhymes.

Masefield, you will note, uplifts you with suggestions of worlds and meanings far beyond the plane of everyday experience. But the typical modern offers no such suggestions whatever. Let us glance at some further examples—none of them extreme—of what has now become the conventional, accepted work:

> I dislike going with a woman
> Into a restaurant. There is
> A plot of mirrors
> All designed to make me self-conscious.
>
> "—Will you
> Please stop looking at yourself
> In your exquisite Cloissonné compact.
> Your lips, your hair is
> Very nice. Everybody's eyes say
> So."
>
> —David Schubert, "Reflections on
> Violence"

> I opened my eyes,
> I looked at the magazine,
> A girl in the magazine crossed her legs at me
> To try to make me buy a cigarette;

I saw the porter coming down the aisle:
Harper's Ferry,
Almost Harper's Ferry . . .
                    —Thomas Hornsby Ferrill, "Harper's
                    Ferry Floating Away"

First are you our sort of a person?
Do you wear
A glass eye, false teeth or a crutch,
A brace or a hook,
Rubber breasts or a rubber crotch,

Stitches to show something's missing? No, no? Then
How can we give you a thing?
Stop crying.
Open your hand. . . .
                    —Sylvia Plath, "The Applicant"

I am dressed in my big shoes and wrinkled socks
And one of the light blue, much-laundered smocks
The men and women of this country wear.
All of us miss our own underwear
And the old days. These new, plain, mean
Days of pain and care, this routine
Misery has made us into cases . . .
                    —Randall Jarrell, "The X-Ray Waiting
                    Room in the Hospital"

my sister drives a green jaguar
my sister has her hair done twice a month
my sister is a school teacher
my sister took ballet lessons
my sister has a fine figure: never diets
my sister doesn't like to teach in Newark
        because there are too many colored
        in her classes
my sister hates loud shades . . .
                    —Le Roi Jones, "Hymn for Lanie Poo'

Percy is my name; my accent is good,
I am told, as good as that of an Elizabethan.
I had no schooling beyond the age of sixteen.
My wife left me. I took to drink, live with a dog.
I resent children unless they can hold their own
With grown-ups. I've been around the world on ships . . .
—Richard Eberhart, "A Maine Roustabout"

Observe that it makes little difference whether the writer resorts to free or conventional forms. Thus Jarrell's passage about his socks and underwear has rhyme and some of the mechanics of meter, but as poetry it is as flat and unrewarding as the other selections. This, of course, is because it contains no poetry and cannot be transmuted into poetry by mere technical devices. And it contains no poetry chiefly because it lacks the imaginative depth, allusions, suggestions, figures, and pictures that have characterized the poetic art in all ages and lands before our own. In other words, it is not creative. And poetry that is not creative is a garden where no seed has ever sprouted.

I do not deny that, even apart from a few outstanding disciples of the older school such as John Masefield and Walter de la Mare, certain twentieth-century poets have given us noteworthy imaginative work. These, however, mainly proceed from poets who achieved recognition several decades ago, or else the authors are sunk in the obscurity that penalizes most rebels against the contemporary trend. By way of comparison with the writers last quoted, here are a few examples:

You have come home with old seas in your speech,
  And glimmering sea-roads meeting in your mind:
The curve of creeping silver up the beach,
  And mornings whose white splendours daze and blind.
—David Morton, "To One Returned from a Journey"

I think October must have loved in vain.
  How otherwise can she portray such grief,

Painting with crimson or with yellow stain
A whole life's story on a falling leaf?
—Joseph Upper, "Artist"

There floats about the fringes of the mind
A music half-remembered, half-divined;
It goes and comes and goes
As the faint fume of a midsummer rose
Wandering through winter fog; it goes and comes
As through the cerements of chrysanthemums
The sea-surge thunders of great Easter wings.
—Geoffrey Johnson, "Intuitions"

I saw the swans fly westward to the hills
In that rich glow the fire of evening brings,
When suddenly a broken shaft of light
Gave all its golden splendour to their wings.

Then for a breathless moment, I beheld
Unearthly beauty in that passing gleam,
Gold birds that flew in golden fields of air
To quiet waters and the hills of dream.
—John Irvine, "The Swans"

I know now how it feels to be a ghost,
Slithering down the chill damp lanes of night,
Blown like the spray along some lonely coast,
Lost in the dark, and vanished in the light;

Pausing to lean against a shutter's lock,
Thinking to enter there and drink a toast . . .
Having no fleshly hand to sound a knock
Or lift a glass to satisfy a ghost;

Turning away—mad for unhaunted sleep . . .
Having no body that a bed could hold,
Having no warm and heavy tears to weep,
Having no age—and being eons old;

Whispering husks of words that rattle—hollow
Whimpering at the thin blue edge of dawn,
Hugging a flame too pale for moths to follow,
Calling your name . . . knowing that you are gone.
—Alexa Lane

Even writers known as modernists now and then do give us
imaginative touches, as when Richard Wilbur says of the death of
the summer that

The field has droned the summer's final mass;
A cricket like a dwindled hearse
Crawls from the dry grass.

This, of course, is traditional despite the irregularity of the last
line. But this is quite out of the contemporary mid-stream. More
frequently, when members of the current school depart from the
down-to-earth manner and the unadulterated prose of John Berryman, Randall Jarrell, and certain others quoted above, they call for
attention with a shout and a flourish, mistaking oddity, shock, con-
tradiction, or incoherence for imagination and originality. They
may, for example, try to jar the reader by unconventional remarks
on nature or the seasons, as did a contributor to a poetry magazine
in referring to "the green outrage of spring." They may take the
rather contemptuous, would-be witty attitude of Kay Boyle:

Spring birds wing to the feeding tray
As Bowery bums wing to a bar.

They may descend even further into the ludicrous, as in James
Dickey's "Fox Blood":

Blood blister over my thumb-moon
Rising, under clear still plastic
Still rising strongly, on the rise
Of unleashed dog-sounds . .

They may resort to profanity, as does Doris Holmes when she remarks in *Saturday Review* that "Hitting my head on the bathroom cabinet/I screech 'God dammit.'" Or they may try for a startling new use of words, as in many of the selections we have examined, and—to offer further examples—in Lionel Wiggam's unconsciously funny "This scene is frozen in a sharp hiatus," and Muriel Rukuyser's meaningless "A man riding on the meaning of rivers," and May Swenson's absurdities of "lofted on sinewy air" and "skinned the mist from the morning," and Louis Simpson's reference to "Poems as progressive as the effect/Of radiation on a foetus," and Jack Hirschman's seriously intended inanities in "Ikon" (Borestone Mountain Poetry Awards, *Best Poems of 1960*): "His howl grabbed me by my high intangibles . . . swaddled a century burning in his thighs . . . Benignly tender zeppelins of a smile."

Expressions such as these, of course, require no imagination, since it is next to impossible to picture what any of them mean. Any jokester, whether a poet or not, can without trouble throw together similar striking-sounding but empty word combinations. For example:

Trepanned the distended cloud-skull.

The diesel of your vapid peregrinations.

The doctor's ministrations in a paleontological intaglio.

Caught the ages in a gargle of aspirin.

But this is not imagination. This is not poetry. This is a mere trick manipulation of phrases in defiance of meaning, in defiance of congruity, in defiance of poetry. Yet such writing not only is common nowadays but has been widely regarded as a substitute for the great imaginative expression which in former days told of "The rushing of the sea-tides of the soul," of "That Light whose smile kindles the Universe," and of man's purpose "To sail beyond the sunset, and the baths/Of all the western stars until I die"—the poetry that took us into the prophetic dreamworld of Byron:

> I had a dream, which was not all a dream.
> The bright sun was extinguish'd, and the stars
> Did wander darkling in the eternal space,
> Rayless, and pathless, and the icy Earth
> Swung blind and blackening in the moonless air . . .

This was the poetry that caused Shelley, in his "Epipsychidion," to conduct us into a world of fantasy whose enchantment has seldom been matched by sober fact:

> There was a Being whom my spirit oft
> Met on its visioned wanderings, far aloft,
> In the clear golden prime of my youth's dawn,
> Upon the fairy isles of sunny lawn,
> Amid the enchanted mountains, and the caves
> Of divine sleep, and on the air-like waves
> Of wonder-level dream, whose tremulous floor
> Paved her light steps;—on an imagined shore,
> Under the gray beak of some promontory
> She met me, robed in such exceeding glory
> That I beheld her not.

Poetry like this, which imaginatively builds out of mist and moonlight to create its own universes, has something to say to a deep and secret part of ourselves. But the supposed imagination of the pseudo-originals shows us nothing but the face of a clown grimacing.

2

Like humor and like genius, imagination comes willy-nilly on the wind, favoring whom it will. It is the possession of children and of creative artists, but it bypasses practical persons, men of affairs, bankers, brokers, businessmen, housewives, and others absorbed in carrying on the material affairs of life. It can be stimulated and developed in those who have it already, but no strain or effort can produce it where nature has not originally planted it. And here is the tragedy of our modern poets, for those without imagination, being blind to their lack and not realizing that it disqualifies them as poets no less than tone-deafness would disqualify them as musicians, try to carry on just as if imagination did not exist. Or else—even worse! —they heave and toss in a mighty endeavor to be or at least to seem imaginative. Thus we will find an unimaginative and hence uncreative line such as Stephen Spender's

I think continually of those who were truly great,

which is hardly in a class with Shelley's

The splendours of the firmament of time,

and is actually no more poetic than Carlyle's prose statement that "We have undertaken to discourse here for a little on great men." Or we come upon Archibald MacLeish's

And the aristocracy of politic selfishness
Bought the land up; bought the towns, the sites,

which, as poetry and on the score of imagination, ranks with "The triumph of individualistic farming was accompanied by the complete divorce of the peasant from the land" (Arthur Birnie, *An Economic History of Europe*), and does not compare with Goldsmith's

One only master grasps the whole domain,
And half a tillage stints thy smiling plain.
No more thy glassy brook reflects the day,
But chok'd with sedges, works its weedy way;
Along thy glades, a solitary guest,
The hollow-sounding bittern guards its nest . .

This, I hasten to add, is far from poetry at its highest flights. But its revealing pictures of the land do illustrate the imaginative as opposed to the unimaginative approach. Unfortunately, the gulf between the two is apparently not recognized by most disciples of the modern school.

Let us suppose, by way of a further example, that a poet decides to write about horses. He may adopt any of several courses. If he has little imagination, he may proceed as does Theodore Holmes in *Poetry* in his "Woman and Horse":

> With foreleg bent in an attitude of supplication,
> On the green of his pasture with head buried in her breasts,
> He is the picture of muscle, sinew, bone, speed
> Tamed by the sweet she holds in her palm.

This is not exceptionally bad, as verse writing goes nowadays; it simply lacks the illuminating flashes that distinguish poetry. To be more precise, it is straight prose.

However, the author would hardly have improved his work if, struggling to supply imagination, he had written:

> Horses . . . strange whirlibeasts
> paroxysms of hooves
> confluence of manes
> caught in the asphyx-
> iation of time
> like a tempest in a thumbnail.

This, of course, is neither imaginative nor original, though it does not exaggerate the antics of the avant-garde as they flounder about for imagination.

Now consider how a modern British poet has dealt with the subject. The following stanzas are from a poem written several decades ago by Edwin Muir and unassumingly entitled "Horses":

> Those lumbering horses in the steady plough,
> On the bare field—I wonder why, just now,

They seemed so terrible, so wild and strange,
Like magic power on the stony grange. . . .

Their conquering hooves which trod the stubble down
Were ritual that turned the field to brown,
And their great hulks were seraphim of gold
Or mute ecstatic monsters on the mould.

And oh the rapture, when, one furrow done,
They marched broad-breasted to the sinking sun!
The light flowed off their bossy sides in flakes;
The furrows rolled behind like struggling snakes.

Here, replete with images and psychological impressions, we have
an imagined re-creation of the horses. Here is something that the
reader can conceive vividly and carry away with him. On the wings
of imagination, the passage has been lifted to poetry.

VIII

BEAUTY, OUTLAW OF THE ARTS

I

If you were to hear a hymn in favor of blindness, an epic in honor of dirt, a paean glorifying meanness and fraud, or an ode exalting stupidity, would you not conclude either that the praise was not meant seriously, or else that you had strayed among lunatics? Yet you would have no reason for greater surprise than when you enter the world of present-day poetry. What now of the beauty that, in the eyes of Keats and many another, was "a joy forever"—"all ye know on earth, and all ye need to know"?

We have already noted in passing that modern poets have, in effect, issued an injunction against beauty, and a mandate on behalf of ugliness. Beauty has been proscribed, along with other stuffy ancient qualities, such as goodness and truth, honor and love; the very word is tabu for poets; it is under condemnation as trite, hackneyed, banal, and therefore passé; it is treated almost as a form of blasphemy. To be sure, this sentence of ostracism against a word might be dismissed as no more than the eccentricity of a clique, were there not also an edict against the spirit represented by the word. Not only must we no longer speak admiringly of beauty; we must not let its malign influence corrupt the poetry of our emancipated century. The mood of too many moderns is that which has been expressed in large capitals by Michael McClure in an anthology,

The New American Poetry: "OH BEAUTY BEAUTY BEAUTY
BEAUTY BEAUTY IS HIDEOUS."

The decline in the appreciation of beauty is suggested, among
other things, by the recent movement to blend poetry and jazz. In
Walter Lowenfels' anthology, *Poets of Today,* Carl Wendell Hines,
Jr., has gone so far as to give us a "jazz poem," with lines such as
"rivers of tears that flow/like gelatin soul-juice" and "paranoidic
peyote visions (or some other source of inspiration)." This jazz
hybridization, originating in the basements of San Francisco, strikes
me as in a class with an attempt to merge the songs of Schubert or
the nocturnes of Chopin with the thump-thump-thump of a tom-
tom. Even though jazz does have rhythm, not all rhythm is that of
poetry, any more than all sounds made on a piano are music. To me
it seems obvious that the excited and exciting tempo of jazz, its evident appeal to the passions, place it as far from the mood and the
beauty of poetry as from the organ blasts of Bach or the *Missa
Solemnis* of Beethoven.

I readily concede that we cannot expect all men to see with the
same eyes—an aborigine in the jungle would not have precisely the
aesthetic reactions of a sophisticated modern in an art gallery. Nonetheless, there are areas in which, by the consensus of mankind, there
has been little or no past disagreement. Thus it has been acknowl-
edged, with no dissent that I have ever heard, that lilies and sunsets
and rainbows and foam-splashed ledges are by their very nature
beautiful. And few have denied the beauty of the sculpture of
Michelangelo, the paintings of Titian, or the symphonies of Mozart
or Brahms. On the other hand, it has been generally accepted that
ash heaps, cesspools, slag piles, slaughterhouses, rags, grime, and dust
are ugly. Only in the borderline area between the beautiful and the
ugly has there hitherto been room for dispute. But nowadays we
have crossed the border; and while the poetry of lilies, sunsets, and
rainbows has been denied, we are asked to accept the poetry of ash
heaps, cesspools, and slag piles, of scars, blotches, blight, and decay.

Take, for example, Allen Ginsberg's notorious "Howl," which
has enjoyed considerable circulation and aroused wide discussion.

Throughout its dozen pages, it is more or less an anthem to the hideous, as represented in lines like the following, which are among the least repulsive:

What sphinx of cement and aluminum bashed open their
    skulls and ate up their brains and imagination?
Moloch! Solitude! Filth! Ugliness! Ashcans and unobtainable
    dollars! Children screaming under the stairways! . . .

Perhaps more characteristic is this passage:

who chained themselves to subways for the endless ride from
    Battery to holy Bronx on benzedrine until the noise
    of wheels and children brought them down shudder-
    ing mouth-wracked and battered bleak of brain all
    drained of brilliance in the drear light of Zoo,
who sank all night in submarine light of Bickford's floated
    out and sat through the stale beer afternoon in deso-
    late Fugazzi's, listening to the crack of doom on the
    hydrogen jukebox . . .

Obviously, this is social protest. But social protest and poetry, though they may meet at the command of the skilled artist, have not necessarily anything in common. Social protest can have elements of beauty, both in form and in expression, as in Margaret Widdemer's *The Factories:*

I have shut my little sister in from life and light,
    (For a rose, for a ribbon, for a wreath across my hair)
I have made her restless feet still until the night,
    Locked from sweets of summer and from wild spring air . . .

But in "Howl," where ugliness dominates both in presentation and in content, one has no intimation that beauty exists even in the broad world beyond the writer's tormented scrutiny. The emphasis is one-sided; the social protest remains, but the poetry is hard to identify.

"Howl," however, is only one example, even if a conspicuous one, of the modern devotion to the cult of antibeauty. In other cases the ugliness is that of descriptive detail, as in the well-known and now almost conservative-sounding lines of T. S. Eliot:

> The winter evening settles down
> With smell of steaks in passageways,

which has been flattered by many imitations, such as K. S. Kennedy's

> You know it's April by the falling off
> In coughdrop boxes.

In the same tradition of "sober realism," we have an effort such as this by Alan Dugan, winner of the 1961 publication award in the Yale Series of Younger Poets:

> the whole flayed lamb stamped
>   QUALITY
> hung by its heels and was
> devoured by a fly. Outside,
> a woman screamed and stopped.
> Two cops came in for coffee-and,
> laughing and filling the place
> with night as black as the sweat
> in the armpits of their shirts.
> "Some guy hit his girl friend.
> And she didn't like it or us
> either."

Or take this from William Carlos Williams' *Paterson:*

> —the leg raised, verisimilitude
> even to the coarse contours of the leg, the
> bovine touch! The leer, the cave of it . . .

Or note this, also from *Paterson:*

> Hell's fire. Fire. Sit your horny ass
> down. What's your game? Beat you
> at your own game, Fire. Outlast you:
> Poet Beats Fire at Its Own Game! The bottle!
> the bottle! the bottle! I
> give you the bottle! What's burning
> now, Fire?

Or witness the opening of "Letter from an Asylum," by Robert Mezey, from his book *The Lovemaker,* which was selected for the 1960 Lamont Poetry Award:

> How can I make you understand, say Argh like
> the balloons of pain in that trash of bullets, tits
> and evacuations, waking up, my goody for grease
> on my temples and numb buzz good morning?

Sometimes the poet goes out of his way to be ugly, shocking, and irreverent all at once, as in Delmore Schwartz' indefensible "Manic-depressive Lincoln, national hero!" and in his offensive grotesquerie, "But it is God, who has caught cold again."

Of an increasingly common type is this by Barbara Moraff, from *Four Young Lady Poets:*

> The name, the haunch, just like by Byron a assy
> Bone, 's cankerous, baring on the castrated pigs
> And cinchonas 's barley-corn I said a human being
> (He can He titi I nose nose something from him)
> The place where he jingle disease, wheat, Einstein;
> Hurtful.

And here, from "The Soft Man," by Gwendolyn Brooks, is a final illustration:

> Disgusting, isn't it, dealing out the damns
> To every comer? Hits the heart like pain.

And calling women (Marys) chicks and broads,
Men hep, and cats, or corny to the jive.
Being seen Everywhere (keeping Alive),
Rhumboogie (and the joint is jumpin', Joe),
Brass Rail, Keyhole, De Lisa, Cabin Inn.
And all the other garbage cans.

Compare this selection with the poetry of Negro life of an earlier colored writer, Claude McKay, as represented, for example, by "The Harlem Dancer." Although the subject is a prostitute, the author somehow rises above grossness to clutch at beauty:

Her voice was like the sound of blended flutes
Blown by black players upon a picnic day.
She sang and danced on gracefully and calm,
The light gauze hanging loose about her form;
To me she seemed a proudly-swaying palm
Grown lovelier for passing through a storm.

Particularly in the concluding lines, the author transcends ugliness with flashes of revelation:

But, looking at her falsely-smiling face
I knew her self was not in that strange place.

It is precisely such redeeming touches that one seeks in vain amid the modern deliberate, unadulterated flouting of beauty.

2

"It was all very well," we will be told, "for the poets of a less complicated age to descant on lily bowers, fabled towers of Camelot, lotus isles, dawns, clouds, and nightingales. But we today live in a stern new era, surrounded less by beauty than by ugliness—ugliness in factories, mines, and streets, in tenements, shops, and battlefields, and in the relationships of man and man. Such ugliness, rather than an imagined beauty, should be portrayed by the poet."

This analysis, unfortunately, is based upon several oversights and distortions. It sees ugliness through magnifying lenses; it takes no account of the fact that much beauty does remain in the modern world, not only in the mists and the mountains, the forests and the seas, and in the more majestic of man's own creations, but in the tenderness and devotion, the love and courage and sacrifice, and at times the heroism of human life. Likewise, the diagnosis builds about a faulty idea of the past. Was it true that the romantics of the early nineteenth century and their Victorian successors inhabited a beauty-dominated world? So far was this from the reality that some of our own festering evils seem, by comparison, of secondary importance. Remember that this was the era of early industrialism, when the overcrowded, pestilential slums of London, Birmingham, Liverpool, and other industrial cities gave forth a stench that was more than physical. Remember also that this was a period of virtual slave labor for working women and pauper children, who drudged on a twelve- or fourteen-hour day for a six-day week (often with additional part-time on Sundays) in disease-breeding factories or still more loathsome mines. Remember, finally, that the poets were not unaware of the conditions: Southey, Kingsley, Matthew Arnold, William Morris, and others appealed in vigorous prose against evils that were not only degrading the population with unspeakable filth and brutality but converting lovely landscapes into wastelands.

Yet this ugliness was comparatively little treated in the poetry of the day. There were indeed, as we shall see in a later chapter, some scattered poetic attempts to attack social problems; but most of these efforts reveal outstanding differences between the nineteenth-century purveyors of ugliness and the twentieth. For example, Gerald Massey (1828–1907), an all-but-forgotten Victorian, excoriated the sordid conditions of his times so bitterly that he could make the narrator in his "The Cry of the Unemployed" express the wish to be dead; yet he could also be optimistic, even to the extent of giving us a poem entitled "The World Is Full of Beauty"—a sentiment inconceivable to the modern, for whom ugliness stands forth in stark blackness in a universe with few if any modulating shades.

It is true that, even in the poetry of the pre-Victorians, ugliness was admitted to have its place, though only in a world wherein it constituted one element out of many. Consider this extract from Spenser's *The Faerie Queene:*

> . . . he sitting found in secret shade
> An uncouth, salvage, and uncivile wight,
> Of griesly hew and fowle ill favoured sight:
> His face with smoke was tand, and eies were bleard,
> His head and beard with sout were ill bedight,
> His cole-blacke hands did seeme to have ben seard
> In smythes fire-spitting forge, and nayles like clawes appeard.

Despite the dream atmosphere, there is not only graphic delineation but a powerful poetic impact in the ghastliness of these often-quoted lines from Shakespeare's *King Richard III:*

> Lord, Lord! Methought what pain it was to drown!
> What dreadful noise of waters in mine ears!
> What ugly sights of death within mine eyes!
> Methought I saw a thousand fearful wrecks,
> Ten thousand men that fishes gnawed upon;
> Wedges of gold, great anchors, heaps of pearl,
> Inestimable stones, unvalued jewels,
> All scattered in the bottom of the sea.
> Some lay in dead men's skulls, and in those holes
> Where eyes did once inhabit there were crept,
> As 'twere in scorn of eyes, reflecting gems,
> Which woo'd the slimy bottom of the deep,
> And mock'd the dead bones that lay scattered by.

Imagination, rhythm, and even beauty amid hideousness characterize this passage and lift it to a level unapproached by any of the modern versified descriptions. Place it beside Howard Nemerov's prosy "I am horrified by the unbridled violence and hostility," or Philip Toynbee's

Irritations! Annoyances! *Itches!* With a prickle in my sweaty
nostrils, tickling toes and eyes wet and dazzled:
His senseless, moist skin where a small fly
Is not afraid of an open, dead eye.

Here, as in some of the previous quotations, we have what may be
called the ugliness of the trivial. How different is the method and
how much more fraught with implications are the lines with which
Poe in "The Conqueror Worm" depicts ugliness of another type:

> Mimes, in the form of God on high,
>   Mutter and mumble low,
> And hither and thither fly—
>   Mere puppets they, who come and go
> At bidding of vast formless things
>   That shift the scenery to and fro,
> Flapping from out their Condor wings
>   Invisible Wo!

A striking example of the skilled poetic use of ugliness has been
provided by Oscar Wilde in "The Ballad of Reading Gaol," where
one of the ghastliest of themes is redeemed from mere prose by the
infusion of beauty, as seen in the vivid pictures, the pervading but
restrained emotion, and the accomplished flow of the rhymed lines.
Perhaps the opening stanzas will serve as well as any in illustration:

> He did not wear his scarlet coat,
>   For blood and wine are red,
> And blood and wine were on his hands
>   When they found him with the dead,
> The poor dead woman whom he loved,
>   And murdered in her bed.
>
> He walked among the Trial Men
>   In a suit of shabby grey;
> A cricket cap was on his head,
>   And his step seemed light and gay;
> But I never saw a man who looked
>   So wistfully at the day.

One does not feel here that fault of overemphasis which marks so many recent writers who make of ugliness the whole of life, somewhat as if they were to describe rosebushes as composed merely of thorns, or honeybees as vicious creatures with stings, who had nothing to do with flowers or nectar. The modern purveyors of ugliness in verse are, of course, in the mid-current of the "realistic" movement in literature. But their realism, I make bold to suggest, often has little relation to reality. By dwelling upon life's seamy side, as in recent sex novels and plays, this so-called realism tends to describe characters and situations distorted out of proper relationship to the world about them; it overstresses exceptional phases of life, until the abnormal and the aberrant appear typical. For this reason, it strikes me that literal and down-to-earth realism is often as far from the truth of life (though in the opposite direction) as Cinderella or Pollyanna.

And if this is a fault in prose, it is a disaster in poetry. While men naturally turn to prose to express the things of every day, poetry has historically been concerned with more vital experience—with man's inner life, his rousing adventures, his dreams, his fantasies, his secret tumults and aspirations, his clutching at meanings and goals denied to the plodder in the street or the shop, his reaching toward the ideal. Hence poetry will be warped and thwarted by too much literalism and by the realism of narrowed or muddied lenses. The result can only be what we have actually seen: the diminishing of poetry, even to the point of nonpoetry.

Let us not forget that, despite all grimness, bleakness, or even hideousness, poetry in the past was dominated by a beauty that sent man's spirit soaring. Such beauty may embody no more than simple, unaffected emotion rhythmically expressed, as in these lines by Christina Rossetti:

> Remember me when I am gone away,
> Gone far away into the silent land;
> When you can no more hold me by the hand,
> Nor I half turn to go yet turning stay.

Or beauty may convey emotion wherein the personal is merged with the universal, as in this from Shelley's "Adonais":

> He is made one with Nature: there is heard
> His voice in all her music, from the moan
> Of thunder, to the song of night's sweet bird;
> He is a presence to be felt and known
> In darkness and in light, from herb and stone . .

In the same mood of quiet reflection, beautiful thoughts on the wings of beautiful expression may give us something like the following, from the sonnet sequence "The Largest Life," by the nineteenth-century Canadian poet Archibald Lampman:

> Nay, never once to feel we are alone,
> While the great human heart around us lies:
> To make the smile on other lips our own,
> To live upon the light in others' eyes. . . .
>
> So to address our spirits to the height,
> And so attune them to the valiant whole,
> That the great light be clearer for our light,
> And the great soul the stronger for our soul:
> To have done this is to have lived, though fame
> Remember us with no familiar name.

Beauty may express itself in a mood of dream-haunted remoteness, as in Tennyson's "Song of the Lotos-Eaters":

> There is sweet music here that softer falls
> Than petals from blown roses on the grass,
> Or night-dews on still waters between walls
> Of shadowy granite, in a gleaming pass,
> Music that gentlier on the spirit lies,
> Than tired eyelids upon tired eyes . . .

The rhyme, the rhythm, and every syllable here reinforce the effect of the sweet, soft music—the lines are themselves sweet, soft music. How can even remotely similar effects be expected from the modern style, as represented, for example, by the contemporary writer Philip Whalen?

F
Train
Absolutely stoned
Rocking bug-eyed billboards *waff*:
No more bridge than adam's
        off ox
            Pouring over it 16 2/3 MPH sodium—
        vapor light yellow light

If it be argued that Tennyson and Whalen did not seek the same ends, the point may be conceded. But one must add that the earlier poet, making use of every tool of poetry, including its beauty, constructed a world that is more real than the alleged realism of the later writer. True, the realm of the lotus-eaters is one of escape, but so is all literature, up to its highest reaches: all literature is escape from the reader's own circumscribed self in favor of creative and sometimes exalted planes.

I cannot help asking how a work such as "The Lotos-Eaters" would appear if translated into the contemporary style. Even if nothing more transforming were done than to abolish the rhyme and rearrange the line lengths, the results would be drastic. With apologies to the shade of Tennyson, I offer this version:

There is sweet
music here
that softer
rests than petals from
blown roses on
the lawn
or night-
dews on still
waters between walls of shadowy
granite in a
gleaming pass.

To read this as poetry is next to impossible, even though the words are Tennyson's except for two substitute nonrhyming line endings. Not only the rhythm but the beauty and the serene effect of the passage have been destroyed by the modernization; the choppy lines impose distractions that make it as hard to read the poem smoothly as it would be, let us say, to be absorbed in Schubert's "Ave Maria" while being bumped over ruts and cobblestones.

Nor is this an extreme example. It is, in fact, very much in the current style, as may be seen, for example, in the following run-of-the-mill bit of modernism which Joel Oppenheimer has contributed to the anthology *A Controversy of Poets:*

> the colors we depend on are
> red for raspberry jam, white
> of the inside thigh, purple as
> in deep, the blue of moods, green
> cucumbers (cars), yellow stripes down
> the pants, orange suns on ill-
> omened days, and black as the
> dirt in my fingernails.

This has, of course, anything but the poetic quality even of our mutilated version of "The Lotos-Eaters." But one suspects that if the moderns were rewriting Tennyson's poem, they would not confine themselves to mere distortions of the lines. One might expect something more in this vein:

> There is rhumba music here
> that hits you like a Molotov cocktail
> or like the pop, pop, popping of bottles
> in a Las Vegas bar
> and shakes your guts out of you
> making your eyelids flop open
> over your rheumy eyes.

But what is beauty? What is the source of its appeal? These questions have been often asked, the more so as few humans, however debased, are without some sense of the beautiful. The caveman showed it in his rock paintings; the wretched slum dweller reveals it in a geranium carefully tended in a window pot. And the poets of the ages, like all artists, have gravitated toward beauty almost as if by instinct. Nor is beauty merely a quality of stars and rivers and mountains, of laughing eyes and dancing gestures and singing lines. Beauty is something that shines through all these but goes beyond all these; it is the illuminated gateway through which one may catch glimpses of the realities beyond the senses.

This fact has been known to the poets. It is in Bryant's mind when, speaking of beauty, he refers in "A Forest Hymn" to

> An emanation of the indwelling Life,
> A visible token of the upholding Love,
> That are the soul of this wide universe.

And it is manifest to Masefield when he writes, in one of his sonnets, of beauty as

> Part of man's store, that lies outside his brain,
> Touch to the dead and vision to the blind,
> Drink in the desert, bread, eternal grain;
> Part of the untilled field that beauty sows
> With flowers untold, where quickened spirit goes.

In another sonnet, Masefield tells us of "This living beauty . . . earth's remembrance of a beauty dead." And whether or not the "living beauty" is indeed "earth's remembrance of a beauty dead," certainly the beauty surviving in the poets of the past offers their best claim to remembrance today. The disturbing fact therefore is that, in most poets of the current school, there is little or no beauty to offer a claim to remembrance tomorrow.

IX

POETS WITH CLOSED EYES

I

"Oh, but he's only a poet! You couldn't expect him to know anything about practical affairs!"

How often do we hear this type of remark, while poets are brushed aside contemptuously, along with infants, morons, eccentrics, and general incompetents? This attitude, of course, takes no account of the many poets who have been in the forefront of important action: Dante, prominent in the political life of his native Florence, and exiled for his political views; Baber (or Babur), who lived from 1483 to 1530, the founder of the Mogul empire in India, a powerful administrator and conqueror, and one of the highest ranking Turki poets; Milton, fighting valiantly for freedom, active for years in public affairs, and serving as Secretary for Foreign Tongues for Cromwell's Commonwealth; André Chenier, a leading French lyric poet of the eighteenth century, guillotined for denouncing the tyranny of Robespierre; and Lamartine, lyric and epic poet, who headed the French Republic in 1848. In our undervaluing of poets, we are widely at variance with the attitudes of many lands and ages, from Homeric Greece through medieval Persia to twentieth-century Latin America and Japan. Why, then, do we downgrade the poet?

In part, undoubtedly, the explanation is to be found in our age, in

its materialistic emphasis, its scientific creeds, and the disillusion-
ments of its turmoils and wars. But in part, it strikes me, the fault
proceeds from the poets themselves. Or, rather, it proceeds from the
dominant school of self-designated poets. In what way do these earn
respect for themselves or for other members of their craft? I am sure
that I too, if I were one of the great majority who have no particular connection with poetry, would look with contempt upon the
authors of supposedly accomplished lines such as

> he's gonna turn out bad/ A J.D./ A Beatnik/ A
> Typical wise-ass N.Y. kid. "X" wanted to bet me . . .

or,

> The pin-swin or spine-swing
> (the edgehog miscalled hedgehog) with all his edges out,
> echidna and echinoderm in distressed-
> pin-cushion thorn-fur coats . . .

Even apart from work such as this, how often do the modernists
among our poets bring a message to the mind and heart? What do
they say to comfort the grieved, soothe the weary, guide the doubt-
ing, exalt the seeker, or shed an illumination as man pursues his
blundering way amid life's shoals and fogs? What vision have they
to offer? What appeal can most of us find in their exhibitionist
struttings and egotistic postures, their assumed objectivity, their pose
of irony toward the struggles and the agonies of mankind, their
flippancies and tricks and trivialities? No breath from the great
world of thought and feeling blows through such an often reprinted
piece as Wallace Stevens' "Sea Surface Full of Clouds," which,
despite its majestic theme of the ocean, is characterized by lines
such as

> In that November off Tehuantepec
> Night stilled the slopping of the sea. The day
> Came, bowing and voluble, upon the deck,

Good clown. . . . One thought of Chinese chocolate
And large umbrellas. . . .

Similarly, no brilliance of a great insight characterizes the much-quoted lines of T. S. Eliot:

Let us go then, you and I,
When the evening is spread out against the sky
Like a patient etherised upon a table.

Personally, I sympathize with the reaction of the British writer C. S. Lewis:

I am so coarse, the things the poets see
Are obstinately invisible to me.
For twenty years I've stared my level best
To see if evening—any evening—would suggest
A patient etherised upon a table;
In vain. I simply wasn't able.

In typical modern realism such as this from Robert Lowell's *For the Union Dead,* we likewise find no dazzling perceptiveness:

You read the *New York Times*
every day at recess,
but in its dry
obituary, a list
of your wives, nothing is news,
except the ninety-five
thousand dollar engagement ring
you gave the sixth.

This lets in about as much light as the average item in today's society columns. Compare this with some of the earlier twentieth-century poems, such as the youthful Edna St. Vincent Millay's "God's World":

O world, I cannot hold thee close enough!
  Thy winds, thy wide gray skies!
  Thy mists, that roll and rise!
Thy woods, this autumn day, that ache and sag
And all but cry with color! that gaunt crag
To crush! to lift the lean of that black bluff!
World, world, I cannot get thee close enough!

This, obviously, is on a plane apart from most recent offerings. And so is Hermann Hagedorn's "Broadway":

How like the stars are these white nameless faces,
  These far innumerable burning coals,
This pale procession out of stellar spaces,
  This Milky Way of souls!
Each in its own bright nebulae enfurled,
Each face, dear God, a world!

On a different level from most current verse, likewise, is Lizette Woodworth Reese's once widely quoted sonnet "Tears," beginning "When I consider life and its few years," and ending with the memorable lines:

Ye old, old dead, and ye of yesternight,
Chieftains, and bards, and keepers of the sheep,
By every cup of sorrow that you had,
Loose me from tears, and make me see aright
How each hath back what once he stayed to weep;
Homer his sight, David his little lad!

Here, as in the best of the older poets, there is vision, there is interpretation, there is a message for the bewildered and sorrowing spirit. But such vision, such interpretation, and such a message are not sought by the typical modern realist, who chooses to work on the external plane and consequently makes no appeal to the depths of man.

This fact was particularly borne home to me when, not long ago,

I made my way through "an anthology of religious poems," *Poems of Doubt and Belief,* edited by Tom F. Driver and Robert Pack. With the exception of some well-known selections by Hardy, Yeats, and a few other representatives of the older generation, I could find little that offered a spiritual lift, spiritual insight, reassurance, wisdom, or faith; the doubt in the poems, it appears to me, is much more conspicuous than the belief. The average inclusion is on the external plane of Howard Nemerov's "Boom! Sees Boom in Religion, Too," which opens thus:

> Here at the Vespasian-Carlton, it's just one
> religious activity after another; the sky
> is constantly being crossed by cruciform
> airplanes, in which nobody disbelieves
> for a second, and the tide, the tide
> of spiritual progress and prosperity
> miraculously keeps rising, to a level
> never before attained. . . .

As mordant social commentary, this may have a place, but obviously it offers nothing for the mind in search of enlightenment. Place this side by side with Emily Brontë's ardent stanzas:

> With wide-embracing love
> Thy Spirit animates eternal years,
> Pervades and broods above,
> Changes, sustains, dissolves, creates and rears.

> Though earth and man were gone,
> And suns and universes ceased to be,
> And Thou wert left alone,
> Every existence would exist in Thee.

> There is not room for Death,
> Nor atom that his might could render void:
> Thou—Thou art Being and Breath,
> And what Thou art may never be destroyed.

You may accept this philosophy or reject it, but you cannot deny that Emily Brontë has a vision which for her is all-sufficient, and which she has done her best to convey on a wave of warm poetic feeling. And this is more than you can say, for example, of a passage such as the following, from Robert Graves' *Collected Poems:*

Fortune enrolled me among the second-fated
Who have read their own obituaries in *The Times,*
Have heard 'Where, death, thy sting? Where, grave, thy vic-
    tory?'
Intoned with unction over their still clay,
Have seen two parallel red-ink lines drawn
Under their manic-depressive bank accounts,
And are therefore strictly forbidden to walk in grave-yards
Lest they scandalise the sexton and his bride.

It is equally hard to see much depth or vision in a poem such as Dylan Thomas' "Altarwise by Owl-Light," in which little if anything is communicated by lines such as

Death is all metaphors, shape in one history;
The child that sucketh long is shooting up,
The planet-ducted pelican of circles
Weans on an artery the gender's strip;
Child of the short spark in a shapeless country
Soon sets alight a long stick from the cradle;
The horizontal cross-bones of Abaddon,
You by the cavern over the black stairs,
Rung bone and blade, the verticals of Adam,
And, manned by midnight, Jacob to the stars.

This sounds as if it might mean something. But precisely what was in the author's mind? Did he himself know? Surely, no probing or transforming emotion could be voiced in such cold tones. And surely, if Thomas had any clear perception, he would have been able to transmit it clearly—would have wanted to transmit it clearly. Compare the above with the certitude and the suggestions of a depth of vision in "Of One Who Seemed to Have Failed," by the American poet S. Weir Mitchell (1829–1914):

> Death's but once more to-morrow. Thou art gray
> With many a death of many a yesterday.
> O yearning heart that lacked the athlete's force,
> And, stumbling, fell upon the beaten course . . .
> Lo, Death, the just, who comes to all alike,
> Life's sorry scales of right anew shall strike.

Or consider the calm and resolute assurance and the evidence of a profound but undemonstrative vision in these stanzas by the eminent American naturalist John Burroughs:

> Serene, I fold my hands and wait,
>   Nor care for wind, or tide, or sea;
> I rave no more 'gainst time or fate,
>   For, lo! my own shall come to me.

> I stay my haste, I make delays,
>   For what avails this eager pace?
> I stand amid the eternal ways,
>   And what is mine shall know my face.

How many contemporary poets could say that they "stand amid the eternal ways"? The truth seems to be that few if any of them believe in any eternal ways. In this they may be right or they may be wrong, but in any case their attitude bears no marks of the vision that has long been the motive power of poetry.

2

Ever since Homer, and probably before, the many-colored pageantry of the natural world has spread in the background of poetry—the panorama of dawns and clouds, rivers and seas, woods and mountains, fields spangled with spring, snowbanks and calm and tempest. Behind this vast stage setting, poets of old have seen stupendous forces at work, intimations of splendors and powers, messages and meanings beyond the senses, in the mood expressed by the American lyric poet Richard Realf (1834–78):

All shapes and sounds have something which is not
Of them: a Spirit broods amid the grass;
Vague outlines of the Everlasting Thought
Lie in the melting shadows as they pass;
The touch of an Eternal Presence thrills
The fringes of the sunsets and the hills.

"I have an understanding with the hills," wrote Grace Hazard Conkling, an American poet of the early twentieth century. "I worshipped the Invisible alone," declared Samuel Taylor Coleridge, as he gazed up at Mont Blanc from the Vale of Chamonix. "The utterance of Eternal thought,/Of which all nature is the speech," the Canadian poet Frederick Scott phrased it. And Wordsworth, in "The Prelude," expressed himself with the fervor of a mystical vision:

While on the perilous ridge I hung alone,
With what strange utterance did the loud dry wind
Blow through my ear! the sky seemed not a sky
Of earth—and with what motion moved the clouds!

Dust as we are, the immortal spirit grows
Like harmony in music . . .

"Like harmony in music" were the thoughts of many of the older bards with reference to nature; like harmony in music, they experienced a vision sometimes deeper than the uttered sound could impart. Such vision, even if imperfectly conveyed, opened up new worlds to the imagination, offered strength and reassurance to the sufferer and the seeker, and underlay a pulse of strong and confident poetry.

This vision, however, is rarely shared by modern writers. They would not hold with Keats that "The poetry of earth is never dead." Reflecting the aloofness and skepticism of the age, they are apt to look upon poetry in the mood of Oscar Wilde, who is said to have remarked with a yawn that the ocean bored him. Nature, truly, seems to bore many moderns. We have seen this in the poems by Stevens and Eliot quoted a few pages back. Equally in a vein of flat disillusionment is Lloyd Frankenberg's

> the ocean goes scotfree
> of other obligation but to pay
> the moon its due respects, discharged like spouse.

In numerous other instances also, the newer writers lower nature to the pits of the ridiculous, as when the widely anthologized young modernist W. D. Snodgrass writes:

> The pear tree lets its petals drop
> Like dandruff on a tabletop

or when Louis Zukofsky, the author of ten books of verse, offers this comparison:

> Zinnias you look so much like Gentiles
> Born among butcher furniture . . .

Hardly more vision or inspiration is shown in a poem such as "Spring Notes from Robin Hill," which Hayden Carruth has contributed to *Poetry:*

> Solomon's Seal and Adder's Tongue,
> Five-leaves, Columbine, Whitlow-grass,
> The misty *Maianthemum canadense,*
> India Cucumber-root and Bluet,
> Saxifrage, Foam-flower, Sweet Cicely,
> Trailing Arbutus, Fumitory . . .
> Rose Marie's Partridge Berry—
> And boo to you, Tom, Dick, and Harry.

In this listing of names in the manner of a seed catalogue, nature is diminished to the level of humdrum. And in much the same way, we find it scorned and degraded in lines such as W. S. Merwin's "And then the day dragged its carcass in back of the hill," and Dylan Thomas' "Over the whirling ditch of daybreak,/Over the sun's hovel." The writers, of course, are entitled to their own perspectives. And so are the authors of shopping lists and of circus advertisements. But this does not make poets of them.

In picturing human life, as in portraying nature, too often the modern poet approaches his theme with a yawn, with an ironic grin, in the mood of John Berryman's "Three Around the Old Gentleman," beginning, "His malice was a pimple down his big/ good face, with its sly eyes." And too often what is taken for character description is a mere enumeration of commonplaces, as in Warren Carrier's "The Talented Wife":

> The man from Mexico, Vienna and New Haven
> Smoked a Mexican cigar. His wife,
> A poet, supplied him with his various pills,
> Packed his bags, drove his car, and otherwise
> Practiced the piano.
>   He translated Nietzsche,
> Composed haiku, painted Cubist miniatures. She
> Wrote long poems, played Bach and Liszt. Together
> They went for hikes, fed their seven cats . . .

To me this sounds like a description by a ten-year-old. Contrast it with the work of a too little remembered English poet of our century, Wilfrid Wilson Gibson, who offers this as one of a series of character descriptions:

ANTHONY EARNSHAW

> We found him sleeping in the drifted snow
> Beside his buried but still breathing ewes.
> 'Tis rarely granted any man, to know
> And find, unsought, the death that he would choose;

Yet he who'd always laboured among sheep
Since he could walk, and who had often said
That death should find him working, stumbled dead
Succouring his flocks, and by them fell asleep.

Spare sinewy body with brown knotted hands
Lean weathered face and eyes that burned so clear
From gazing ever through the winds that blow
Over wide grassy spaces, one who stands
Beside you, quiet on your hurdle-bier,
Envies your hard-earned death amid the snow.

Here is the vision that penetrates. Here, in epitome, is a life story.
Here, too, is realism—but realism that does not rule out a subjective
view. And here is poetry.

3

We have all known the man who sees life as composed of facts
and figures, of banknotes and statistics, furniture and rugs, accounts
payable and accounts paid, automobiles and television sets and deep
freezers. We have also known, even if more rarely, the man who
finds the world not to be what it seems, who perceives in a human
being not a mere complex of muscles and nerves but a throbbing,
impalpable entity inhabiting a world of invisible forces and moving
toward unseen and even magnificent ends.

The first man is the ordinary nose-to-earth plodder down path-
ways of prose. And the second, though not necessarily a poet, is the
person of poetic vision. Only from his mind can creative literature
arise. Yet which of the two is most honored today and most encouraged as a poet?

The answer is blared forth in scores of the selections we have
examined. It is proclaimed, to take another example, by "Definition
in Blue," recently contributed by the American writer John Ashbery
to *The Literary Supplement* of the London *Times*. I quote the
opening lines:

The rise of capitalism parallels the advance of romanticism
And the individual is dominant until the close of the nineteenth century.
In our own time, mass practices have sought to submerge the
personality
By ignoring it, which has caused it to branch out in all directions . . .

Place this side by side with the following:

As the nineteenth century advanced and as the anti-Jacobin
spirit receded,
Humanitarianism invaded one province of life after another,
Softening the rude and often brutal temper of the past,
And fostering instead a cheerful benevolence of heart some-
times running to sentimentality.

Would you not say that the two selections were about equal for
vision and poetic quality? Yet the second, which I have rearranged
to look like poetry, is from the prose of G. M. Trevelyan (*Illustrated
English Social History,* Vol. IV).

To be sure, the author of the first piece has much recent so-called
poetic precedent behind him. In his inclination to see the world in
terms of prosy facts and figures, he can point to eminent characters,
including William Carlos Williams, Wallace Stevens, and Marianne
Moore. He can even cite the dean of the moderns, T. S. Eliot, who
has moved in the same mood of dry, unilluminated philosophy in
various offerings, including "Four Quartets" and "Gerontion," with
lines like these:

                                        Think how
History has many cunning passages, contrived corridors
And issues, deceives with whispering ambitions,
Guides us by vanities. Think now
She gives when our attention is distracted
And what she gives, gives with such supple confusions
That the giving famishes the craving. . . .

Printed as prose in the pages of an A. J. P. Taylor or an Arnold Toynbee, this might not seem out of place. One will not deny that it has a vision of a sort, though unfortunately not the vision of the poet. It is hardly in a class with the lines on the same subject by a little-known American poet of this century, Robert Morse:

> The past keeps watch above the present's sleep,
> and sits all night in judgement on itself.

It is by no means to be ranked with these lines on a similar theme by the almost forgotten English poet William Robert Spencer (1769-1834):

> How noiseless falls the foot of Time,
> That only treads on flowers!
>
> What eye with clear account remarks
> The ebbing of the glass,
> When all its sands are diamond sparks,
> That dazzle as they pass!

Least of all is the passage from Eliot of the same genus as these well-known lines of Blake:

> To see the world in a Grain of Sand,
> And a Heaven in a Wild Flower,
> Hold Infinity in the palm of your hand,
> And Eternity in an hour.

Here is the typical insight of the poet. And here, in four lines, the writer utters himself with a memorable quality impossible to the man without poetic vision.

This typical poetic insight has inspired many writers of mystical verse, including the American lyric and dramatic poet Cale Young Rice, who in his "Atavism" reports an unusual vision of the sea:

> And I felt old stirrings wake in me, under the tides of time,
> Sea-hauntings I had brought with me out of the ancient slime.

And now, as I muse, I cannot rid my senses of the spell
That in a tidal trance all things around me drift and swell
Under the sea of the Universe, down into which strange eyes
Keep peering at me, as I peered, with wonder and surmise.

On the wings of a soaring mystical insight, the Irish poet "A.E."
has given us the essence of a whole idealistic philosophy:

> Only from dream to dream our spirits pass
> Well, let us rise and fly from sphere to sphere;
> Some one of all unto the light more near
> Mirrors the Dreamer in its glowing glass.

From the simplest things of the earth blossoms the vision of the
poet, as in Edna St. Vincent Millay's "Renascence," which opens
with the observation of "three long mountains and a wood" and
"three islands in a bay," and goes on to the discovery that

> The world stands out on either side
> No wider than the heart is wide;
> Above the world is stretched the sky,—
> No higher than the soul is high.
> The heart can push the sea and land
> Farther away on either hand;
> The soul can split the sky in two,
> And let the face of God shine through.

Note that all this is described in the simplest, most unostentatious
phrases. There is no attempt to dazzle with striking expressions, no
"icicles on bicycles play iceBall games" (to quote Frank Polite in
Poetry), no "He lolls in the stink of blistering old lino" (Stanley
Cook, in the *London Times Literary Supplement*), nothing in the
vein of "My soul, like some heat-maddened fly/Keeps buzzing at the
sill" (Theodore Roethke, "In a Dark Time"). Nevertheless, we have
vision—and we have poetry. One may add that the vision has made
the poetry. But one may also add that any attempt to startle or excite
could have unmade the vision.

X

WORSHIPPERS AT
THE TEMPLE DOOR

I

There was a young poet named John, who wished always to think, say, and do what was exactly right. Fortunately, this was not hard, since John had only to walk in the footsteps of his friends, neighbors, and teachers. Whether he really believed in their all-wisdom, I cannot say; but if a majority proclaimed that black was white, then John would blink and assert that he had always known that black is white. And if a majority held that the clattering of tin cans was music, then John would shout that he recognized Mozartian melodies amid the clangor. This readiness to side with the majority, of course, made John very popular. It also put him in the avant-garde movement in poetry.

In the course of the years, I have known a number of Johns, along with their feminine counterparts. Their characteristics are always the same. Although they would piously shrink from any idea not handed over to them by their preceptors and associates, they speak out with a devout faith in the rightness of their views—that is, until those views are changed by a vote of the authorities. Their position, accordingly, as they gather about the temple door to hear the commandments of the high priests of poetry, is the typical one of the religious believer. Like other religious believers, they can rarely be persuaded by argument. Just as rarely can they be induced to disobey the dictates of the gods.

What chiefly rules them, however, is the series of officially approved assumptions and dogmas which, like those of other religions, are accepted on trust and followed with unquestioning obedience. Inevitably, those assumptions and dogmas govern their writing and their views of the writing of others, and so are important for an understanding of what has been happening in poetry.

2

Some time ago a critic, trying to judge whether a certain particularly disordered bit of work was poetry, decided in the affirmative, his reason being that it gave a perfect imitation of a drunkard in a barroom. This made it evident that the critic accepted the first of the dogmas and assumptions of the new religious believers: *You can write poetry on any subject whatever.*

Now this idea is not wholly new, nor is it exclusively a product of the West. Something similar has cropped up under communism in Russia. George Bailey, writing in *The Reporter* on "The Trial of Two Soviet Writers," has expressed the situation:

> Because of the imperative need to transmute the value of labor experience into poetic values, the function of the poet must be to certify the activities of all other worker-contributors to Communism. This has led a number of workers—both skilled and unskilled—to mistake job description for literary production, avowedly in the belief that if a worker eulogizes his work in verse he is of necessity a poet. The result has been insuperable confusion.

The result, wherever the poet's subject matter is picked for reasons unrelated to poetry, must be "insuperable confusion."

This has been proved long before our time—as much as a century or two ago, when enthusiasm for newly sprouting science and industry led poets to expand upon novel themes, sometimes in their ardor producing gems such as

Inoculation, heavenly Muse divine!

In the work of Erasmus Darwin (1731–1802), the grandfather of Charles Darwin and himself a scientist and an evolutionist of repute, we see the new tendency to extend poetry to all themes in lines such as

Hail, Adamantine Steel, magnetic Lord!
King of the prow, the plowshare, and the sword!

Typical was this exaltation of the black mineral:

—Sable Coal his massy couch extends,
And stars of gold the sparkling pyrite blends;
—Dull-eyed Naphtha pours his pitchy streams,
And Jet uncoloured drinks the solar beams . . .

It would be rash to suggest that good poetry could not have been written on these themes. But it remains true that no good poetry was written, and that some of Erasmus Darwin's verses now sound slightly ridiculous. Yet here was a precedent for the moderns.

A more conspicuous precedent was provided by Walt Whitman, who tended to be least poetic precisely when he was most expansive in theme, although the range of his subject matter was much less than has been attempted by his successors. Thus, although he shocked some of his readers by his treatment of sex, he nowhere approaches the freedom of expression or the bad taste—or, more accurately, the lack of all taste—of some of our own contemporaries. But more daring innovations were introduced in the early twentieth century, as when Carl Sandburg came forth with his description of Chicago, "hog-butcher for the world," and when Edgar Lee Masters startled literary circles with his *Spoon River Anthology*, which gave brief, varied, and often unsavory sketches of the lives of the inhabitants of a small town; his theme is summarized in these lines:

Where are Elmer, Herman, Bert, Tom, and Charley,
The weak of will, the strong of arm, the clown, the boozer,
    the fighter?
All, all, are sleeping on the hill.

One passed in a fever,
One was burned in a mine,
One was killed in a brawl,
One died in a jail . . .

To an extent this represented innovation, although it verged toward nonpoetry, as was also true of some of Masters' work outside the *Spoon River Anthology,* including the long poem *Domesday Book,* with lines such as these:

> An inquisition taken for the people
> Of the State of Illinois here at LeRoy,
> County aforesaid, on the 7th of August,
> Anno Domini, nineteen hundred nineteen,
> Before me, William Merival, coroner
> For the said County, viewing here the body
> Of Elenor Murray, lying dead upon
> The oath of six good lawful men . . .

This, if anything, is even less poetic than the versified science of Erasmus Darwin. But this is significant in that Masters has helped to apply the fuse to the more recent explosion in subject matter, handing down the principle, "You can write poetry on any subject whatever." Very much in the Masters mood is the following, from T. S. Eliot's "Coriolan":

> . . . The companions of the Bath, the Knights of the British
>   Empire, the Cavaliers,
> O Cavaliers! of the Legion of Honour,

The Order of the Black Eagle (1st and 2nd class),
and the Order of the Rising Sun.

Poetically, this is in a class with

. . . The Outfielders of the White Sox, the Umpires of the
American League, the Pinch-Hitters,
O Pinch-Hitters! and champion run-getters,
The Order of the New York Yankees (1st and 2nd Basers)
And the Order of the Los Angeles Dodgers.

But elsewhere Eliot goes far beyond Masters. What would you
say of the following, also from "Coriolan"?

5,800,000 rifles and carbines,
102,000 machine guns,
28,000 trench mortars,
53,000 field and heavy guns,
I cannot tell how many projectiles, mines and fuses,
13,000 aeroplanes,
24,000 aeroplane engines,
50,000 ammunition waggons,
now 55,000 army waggons,
11,000 field kitchens,
1,150 field bakeries.

It is hard to see how, in any form or with any treatment whatever,
this arithmetical enumeration could be classified as poetry. As given
above, it has hardly the poetic quality of a Montgomery Ward cata-
log, and not more than the artistic attainment of a table of loga-
rithms. One might as well represent the following, from this morning's stock reports, as modern poetry:

A

Abbot Lab 1	39	$43\frac{1}{8}$	43	$-\frac{1}{8}$
ABC Con .80	65	$27\frac{7}{8}$	27	$-\frac{5}{8}$
ACF Ind 1.80	40	$50\frac{1}{4}$	50	$-1\frac{1}{4}$
Acme Mt 2b	9	$49\frac{3}{4}$	50	$+\frac{1}{4}$

Not many writers, it is true, go quite to such extremes, though many do move in the same direction by a listing of names, places, and figures, as in a number of the cases we have observed. Or take this relatively mild instance, from *Nothing Is a Wonderful Thing,* by Helen Wolfert:

> And Ezekiel Kahn sits in his chair,
> Son of Solomon, Ben Chaim Kahn,
> Grandson of Rabbi Chaim Kahn,
> Great-grandson of Rabbi Ezekiel Kahn,
> Who sprang from Solomon Kahn.

It happened one night that a neighbor of mine—a businessman who makes no poetic claims—picked up a book from my library table, opened at the lines quoted above, and began silently to read. After a few seconds his face lit up; within half a minute he was roaring with laughter. "But where is the poetry?" he asked, after sufficiently recovering from his merriment. "*Where* is the poetry?" And I must confess that I was hard pressed to find an answer. It was no use to assure my visitor that the passage was no more unpoetic than hundreds, even thousands, published in recent years; that its subject matter was no further from poetry than is common in sophisticated circles. I tried hard to convince him that this work was intended with the most unsmiling seriousness. But all to no avail. Every time he glanced again into the book and was also regaled by expressions like "Whoops! Whoopee! Hoopla!"—he would go off into peals of merriment. The climax came when he asked to borrow the book for the amusement of some of his dinner guests, who, he laughingly asserted, were not well enough acquainted with the modern Muse.

Let us go on to another case. Here are some characteristic lines from Karl Shapiro's *Essay on Rime:*

> I do not here attempt the definition
> Of rime, which is the province of esthetics,
> But to point out its ratio to language.

> In the mathematical sense, rime is a power,
> Prose raised to the numerical exponent
> Of three or six or even *n,* depending
> Upon the propensity of the literature
> At a particular time and on the bent
> Of the particular poet. . . .

One's immediate reaction is, "But this is the subject matter and the method of prose!" And this reaction is confirmed if one takes the trouble to rearrange the lines in the form of prose:

> I do not here attempt the definition of rime, which is the province of esthetics, but to point out its ratio to language. In the mathematical sense, rime is a power, prose raised to the numerical exponent of three or six or even *n,* depending upon the propensity of the literature at a particular time and on the bent of the particular poet.

By way of comparison, read the following, from Theodore Maynard's prose work, *Preface to Poetry:*

> Rhyme is no more than a device designed to heighten poetic perception. Incidentally it is an invaluable aid to the memory, but though critics now and then defend it on that score, that is not why poets use it. They use it as a net to capture the elusive muse.

While this is no more than the prose that the author intended, is it at all fantastic to suggest that it is closer to poetry than Karl Shapiro's blank verse?

Then where does the difficulty lie? Can it be traced wholly to the choice of subject matter? Would it not be possible for an accomplished writer to create poetry on this theme? Alexander Pope, in *An Essay on Criticism,* has furnished an answer:

> True ease in writing comes from art, not chance,
> As those move easiest who have learn'd to dance.

> 'Tis not enough no harshness gives offence,
> The sound must seem an Echo to the sense:
> Soft is the strain when Zephyr gently blows,
> And the smooth stream in smoother numbers flows;
> But when loud surges lash the sounding shore,
> The hoarse, rough verse should like the torrent roar:
> When Ajax strives some rock's vast weight to throw,
> The line too labours, and the words move slow;
> Not so, when swift Camilla scours the plain,
> Flies o'er th' unbending corn, and skims along the main.

Admittedly, this does not scale the peaks of inspiration. Nevertheless, few will deny that it is poetry. Yet its subject matter—a critique of poetic method—is not far from that which Karl Shapiro handles so prosily.

While it should be self-evident that not every subject is suitable for poetry, while one could not express a chemical reaction, a mathematical formula, nor even all the routine details of life in poetic form, we do not as a rule recognize that there are wide areas of modern experience which are susceptible to poetic treatment and yet are generally neglected by our poets. To this subject we shall return in a later chapter. But first let us consider some other current dogmas and assumptions.

3

There was once, we are told, a poet who recited his verses while standing on his head or while dancing naked on his apartment roof, thereby insuring himself a degree of attention not always accorded to the best bards—that is, until the police inconsiderately put an end to his performances. This poet, of course, was being faithful to one of the prime modern assumptions or dogmas: *Poetry should be novel, and never hackneyed or trite.*

In this case, to be sure, the poet rather than the poetry was assuming a novel and unhackneyed attitude. But, after all, it is often hard to distinguish between the two. Our unorthodox roof performer was really in line with some famous predecessors who sought novelty through exhibitionism, as when the California poet Joaquin Miller drew attention to himself by appearing at the Court of St. James in high boots and a cowboy's outfit. It is merely a matter of personal preference that leads many poets to seek the novelty in their verses rather than in their lives.

But why should they not try to be novel, and to avoid hackneyed and trite expressions? No one, presumably, would lay down the commandment, "Thou shalt not be novel!" or "Thou shalt be hackneyed and trite!" The danger occurs only when the poet makes a goal of novelty, to the neglect of poetry, and when the rules become so formalized as to be themselves trite and hackneyed. Certainly not poetic license, nor any other kind of license, including the license to be novel, can entitle the prose writer to abandon the laws of the logical relationships of things and to associate such matters as symphonies and radishes, love trysts and decimal systems, or ballets and the digestive functions of spiders. Nor can poetic license, nor any other kind of license, justify the poet in abandoning rhyme, rhythm, and reason in pursuit of the merely novel in the way that we have observed time after time, not only forsaking a rational sequence of thought but in many cases irrelevantly introducing foreign or shocking phrases and offering no more than a disintegrated or nonsensical prose. Not poetic license, nor any other kind of license —to cite a specific further case—can condone the sort of novelty presented by Martha Hazzard Mayer when, in a recent poem in *The Christian Century,* she declares:

> And in the bone-weary nights,
> The minister's wife cried for the loose stars in the sewer.

It is safe to say that, outside of this effort at poetry, no minister's wife or anyone else's wife, unless suffering from extreme dissociation of the personality, ever cried for "the loose stars in the sewer." Yet such decomposition of language and such dishonoring of thought have been offered not only in the words of multitudinous obscure aspirants but, as we have seen, by some of the better known writers such as Pound and Cummings, or such as John Ciardi, who opens his "For Ezra Pound" with these lines:

> Bagged for glory, then—a goat saint lolling
> satyr drunk and smiling loose-lipped
> Heavens and Earths, the eyes rolling
> ecstasy and maunder, the beard flipped
> to glory and wattle visible under it. Die
> (giggle) dying (giggle) but not yet dead
> (by a damn sight) not dead yet (sigh)
> but only cracked and queer with a head
> full of the reasons for wine, that tomb-taste
> in the lees, a most like-life. . . .

Here again nothing is trite. Nothing is hackneyed. And nothing has much more relation to poetry than to the star Sirius.

Yet such work generally receives the commendation of critics. A case in point was to be seen when James Schevill, director of the San Francisco Poetry Center, in February, 1966, published a newspaper review in which he found "a capacity for the fresh penetrating image" in lines that included the following from David Ray's *X-Rays* (Cornell University Press):

> With deathlace tickling my throat
> I'm bulb-eyed at midnight
> To remember whole afternoons of causes. . . .
> The expressways, with their share
> For each tax payer, share of the modern death.
> These are the death-flies hovering
> Around my curls, sneaking a bite
> At my tense neck of Apollo . . .

But this is almost conservative compared with some recent departures. Note this item from *The New York Times Book Review* for December 5, 1965, regarding A. R. Ammons' *Tape for the Turn of the Year* (Cornell University Press):

. . . a "long thin poem"—written over the course of a month on a roll of adding-machine tape which determines its length and width—"a kind of Orphic encephalogram, attached to a poet who is composing 24 hours a day." Far from being a stunt, "it is supple, immensely witty, and even readable. What else do you want?"

"What else do you want?" No doubt I am but one of a small, out-of-date minority, but I want poetry. Suppleness, wit, readability, these are all estimable qualities, yet these are possessed by many a work, from *Gulliver's Travels* to *Candide* and from *Huckleberry Finn* to *Androcles and the Lion,* which have never been represented to us as anything but prose. Suppleness, readability, and wit do not in themselves bring us even to the outskirts of poetry. What, therefore, are we to make of the fact that a great university press can treat them as poetically sufficient, while a critic for a leading review can add his evident approval? To my mind, this not only shows the depth of the current confusion as to poetry, but indicates how completely we have lost sight of the nature of the art, how bemused we have become with the cult of novelty, and how blind this has made us to the distinction between poetry and its counterfeit.

The conscientious poet does, of course, try when possible to avoid overworked expressions ("clichés," a word so overused as to have become itself a cliché). He will not speak of a "gentle breeze" or of a "rushing river" if he can substitute a more graphic, equally truthful phrase; he will not say that a man has "an axe to grind" if he can think of something fresher to describe ulterior motives. Yet I, for one, would prefer a "rushing river" to "an expressway genus sub-Amazon," which would be more novel but might distract my attention and leave me in doubt as to the meaning. I would rather hear it stated that a man had an axe to grind than be confused by being told with untrite originality that he had "cross-grained motivations precipitated by razored incongruities of interest."

Modern poets, in stressing the perils of clichés, fail to see that they may be emphasizing the mere minutiae of a poem at the expense of its more significant features and even to the neglect of the spirit of the whole—after all, a poem is more than an aggregation of its parts. They forget that a poem may have a good overall effect even when it contains phrases frequently used. We have seen this in Wordsworth's "She dwelt among the untrodden ways." A more recent example is John Hall Wheelock's "Earth," beginning with these unassuming lines:

> Grasshopper, your tiny song
> And my poem alike belong
> To the dark and silent earth,
> From which all poetry has birth . . .

It may be objected that "tiny song" has been used before, and that "dark and silent earth" is common and unoriginal. Yet these simple words make it possible for the author to say what he wishes without strain, and to obtain the effect he desires. Would the poem be improved if transcribed in the modern style, avoiding the trite by the use of more novel expressions?

> Grasshopper, your jazzy song,
> Whirr, whirr, whirr, whirr,
> Is made, like my poems, in the professional parlors
> Of the dumb mortician earth,
> Which gives all poetry a private first audition.

Possibly this will seem original. Unfortunately, it not only eliminates rhyme and meter but changes the meaning and the effect. "Tiny" and "jazzy" are by no means the same; while if anything is certain about poetry it is that it is not given "a private first audition" in the professional parlors of a mortician, whether dumb or not. But what matter? The revised version avoids clichés.

Doubtless it is dread of the bugaboo of clichés that mainly accounts for the distorted phrases we have noted—phrases such as, to mention further examples, Harold Witt's "Squirrelfaced Shelley" (whose accuracy may be strongly challenged), Gwendolyn Brooks'

"Whose janitor javelins epithet and thought/To cheapen hyacinth darkness that we sought," and Ted Hughes' "The death of a gnat is a star's mouth," and "Those stars are the flesh forebears/Of these dark hills," and "My skull burrows among antennae and fronds"—in all of which we can see no clichés, even though gnats and stars and skulls are forced into acrobatic contortions that neither fact nor poetry ever asked of them before.

Compare these expressions with the older simplicities, as represented, let us say, by the celebrated lines of Robert Herrick, who probably never gave a thought to what was and what was not hackneyed:

> Gather ye rosebuds while ye may,
>   Old Time is still a-flying:
> And this same flower that smiles to-day
>   To-morrow will be dying.

Three centuries have passed since this stanza was written, but somehow it has not lost its freshness. I question whether, a few hundred years hence, anything similar will be said of unhackneyed modern lines such as, for example, these by Robert Creeley in *Poetry:*

> My voice is
> a foot. My
> head is
>
> a foot.

And I doubt if men in the twenty-third century will recall untrite work such as John Crowe Ransom's "Survey of Literature":

> In all the good Greek of Plato
> I lack my roastbeef and potato.
>
> A better man was Aristotle,
> Pulling steady on the bottle.

I dip my hat to Chaucer,
Swilling soup from his saucer.

And to Master Shakespeare
Who wrote big on small beer.

4

An acquaintance of mine calls himself a progressive and even a radical in politics and economics. He also thinks of himself as a progressive and radical in poetry. He sees much that, in his view, should be repaired in our social system; hence he concludes that much should be repaired in everything, poetry included. This is a position that I have never been able to appreciate. "But, George," I would argue—George, by the way, is not actually his name—"even if you are right in feeling that migrant farm laborers are abused or that sharecroppers need a new freedom of opportunity, it does not follow that we must have a new freedom in poetry. Why isn't it possible for you to be a social reformer and at the same time a literary conservative?"

But George would only shake his head, stare across at me with a look of slightly pitying condescension, and answer, with an air of unshakable conviction, "Ah, but you don't see. I believe in progress —progress in everything. I hold that poetry must move forward with the times!"

In these words, he stated, though perhaps without realizing it, the third of the poetic assumptions and dogmas of the day: *Poetry must move forward with the times.* This has been the implicit belief behind the "modern movement" ever since Harriet Monroe in 1912 launched her celebrated *Poetry: A Magazine of Verse.* Nothing, of course, could seem more harmless than this precept—everyone is automatically in favor of progress, just as everyone is in favor of "mother," "goodness," and "justice." The only room for debate is in regard to interpretation—just what do we mean by "moving forward with the times"? I am certain, for example, that my friend George and I would have different answers to this question. While I am as strongly for progress as he is, I do believe that the idea has been overemphasized and misinterpreted ever since Darwin and indeed ever since the eighteenth century, until we have taken it for granted that everything in human life has to move forward, and has to move forward at about the same speed and with progress of the same brand and variety.

I will concede that few things in life can remain static: nonmotion is likely to mean petrifaction. But to state this is not to specify what kind of change is desirable. Poetry, we should remember, has been building a magnificent tradition in the West for three thousand years; in the English-speaking world, many consummate creations have been woven on the trellis of an evolved technique since Chaucer and even before. Perfection is not a word that one should use lightly, yet some of the more inspired passages by our poets approach as near to complete mastery of content and method as seems humanly possible. Take, for example, these stanzas from Coleridge's "The Ancient Mariner":

> All in a hot and copper sky,
> The bloody Sun, at noon,
> Right up above the mast did stand,
> No bigger than the Moon.
>
> Day after day, day after day,
> We stuck, nor breath nor motion;
> As idle as a painted ship
> Upon a painted ocean.

Mark the consummate craftsmanship of this from Tennyson's "Tears, Idle Tears," in which blank verse is used as rarely before or since:

> Ah, sad and strange as in dark summer dawns
> The earliest pipe of half-awaken'd birds
> To dying ears, when unto dying eyes
> The casement slowly grows a glimmering square;
> So sad, so strange the days that are no more.

For vividness of portrayal, few compositions have ever surpassed Shelley's "Prometheus Unbound." And this statement applies not only to dreamlike passages such as

> My soul is an enchanted Boat,
> Which, like a sleeping swan, doth float
> Upon the silver waves of thy sweet singing . . .

Even more does this characterization pertain to descriptions of strife and turmoil, such as

> An eagle so, caught in some bursting cloud
> On Caucasus, his thunder-baffled wings
> Entangled in the whirlwind, and his eyes
> Which gazed on the undazzling sun, now blinded
> By the white lightning, while the ponderous hail
> Beats on his struggling form, which sinks at length
> Prone, and the aërial ice clings over it.

Above all, as an expression of resolution and courage, observe the poem's concluding lines:

> To suffer woes which Hope thinks infinite;
> To forgive wrongs darker than death or night;
> To defy Power, which seems omnipotent;
> To love, and bear; to hope till Hope creates
> From its own wreck the thing it contemplates;
> Neither to change, nor falter, nor repent;
> This, like thy glory, Titan, is to be
> Good, great and joyous, beautiful and free;
> This is alone Life, Joy, Empire, and Victory.

Although this passage lacks the varicolored imagery of much of Shelley, it is hard to see how it could be surpassed as a proclamation of unflinching courage and heroic resolve. It is important to note, moreover, that the unflinching courage and heroic resolve are reinforced by the rhyme and emphasized by the rhythm. In what direction, therefore, could we progress from such work? When the climber has at last struggled to the peak, there is only one way in which he can go.

Not that there have been no conspicuous advances in poetry before Shelley and after. As I shall return to this subject in the concluding chapter, it will suffice at this point to mention that enormous gains were made in English poetry so far back as Chaucer and later by Chaucer's successors, including Shakespeare and the other Elizabethan dramatists and songwriters, along with Milton, Shelley, Pope, Swinburne, and many others. These advances, however, represented no denial of the past but rather growth from old roots, while the improvements in technique were secondary to the developments in the spirit and content of the poetry.

This is not to suggest that every stone added to the mansion of poetry by every traditional writer has necessarily been sound. Human evolution normally proceeds in zigzags rather than in straight lines, and poetry has been no exception. Not always have even the best traditional poets scaled the summits; too often they have repeated themselves in theme and artifice; too often there are padded and prosy passages even in the leaders, from Dryden and Pope to Wordsworth, Browning, and Tennyson.

But this should not keep us from seeing that the faults of the older poetry were decried as faults rather than hailed as attainments; nor should it disguise the fact that the superb edifice of English poetry could have been erected by no one craftsman and no single group but only by a long, inspired succession of workers. Nor should we fail to note that the revolt in modern poetry is primarily not a progressive movement but a rebellion against progress. In abandoning clarity, communicated emotion, simplicity, rhythm, beauty, imagination, and meaning, some of the key figures among the insurgents and droves of their followers have placed themselves squarely against the forward-looking movements of centuries. Under the banners of radicalism, though they themselves would be the last to admit it, they have given us antiprogress.

XI

CLEAR WATER FROM
MUDDY SPRINGS?

I

A peculiar legend persists in regard to the poet. He is pictured as a man of Gargantuan appetites and unlimited licentiousness, who pours down wine, whisky, and vodka like water, seduces the girls of the neighborhood with the sedulousness of a Don Juan, and is more likely than not to be given to narcotics, homosexuality, and other vices. At the same time, he is a creature of happy-go-lucky moods, whose signature on a check is hardly to be trusted, and who works by fits and starts and then only when the mood suits him (which isn't very often). But this devil-may-care Bohemian, this irresponsible sensualist, is given credit for a great creative gift, which operates with a sort of automatic spontaneity and enables him to produce all that passes for poetry in our age.

The view of the poet is exactly on the level of the myth of the banker who spends most of his days fishing in the Bahamas or yachting in the South Seas, while scheming how to pass forged checks legally or how to turn out counterfeit bills without brushing against the law. Just as such a man could never be a brilliant financial light, so the frenzied and debauched poetic genius, as popularly conceived, is not likely to rank high among literary creators. In both cases alike, the man's character would forbid preeminent accomplishment.

Character is of first importance among poets, even as among bankers, statesmen, clergymen, and clerks. If the spring is muddied, a man cannot draw pure water from it; if his mind is warped or twisted, he cannot see or act with the straightforwardness of a clear vision. In the poetic field, as in all fields, these are paramount facts. And these are facts that, more than any other, will explain the curious phenomena we have observed, the poses, gestures, pretenses, distortions, aberrations, and sheer absurdities that have pockmarked one of the most glorious of the arts as with the pustules of a mortal disease and threaten to blot out its fair face entirely.

Let me cite a few examples—examples of poets I have known. There was one whom I will call Joe. When I first met him, years ago, he was a dedicated man, with a faraway glitter in his eyes; he earned his living, as so many must, at a humdrum job, but all his spare time was given to poetry. To him it was a love, a consecration; he devoured the poetry in books and in the world about him; he wrote of nature and man with ardor, almost with passion. To me, as to others in his small circle, he seemed to show rare promise. True, his poems were accepted only by a few obscure magazines; true, publishers were not interested in a volume of his verses, while a slender self-financed book, which appeared under an unknown imprint, failed to attract any attention. But this is the lot of many; Joe was still young, and we who admired his work thought that he might yet become a standard-bearer of American poetry.

After a time, however, a change came over Joe. Hitherto a traditionalist, he laid siege to one or two of the country's best-known verse writers, who happened not to be traditionalists. He did service at their doorsteps, he courted them, he minced and fawned before them, he flattered them, he wrote poems of adulation to them, and gradually he maneuvered his way into their favor, even inducing one of them to write an introduction to his second book. At the same time, he dropped his old friends, the conservative poets, including those to whom he was most indebted. During the same general period, he gave up his job, being prepared, as he said, to live from hand to mouth; and simultaneously he changed his style of writing.

He discarded rhyme, or else used it in unconventional ways; he abandoned his previously smooth rhythms; he sought shocking, jarring effects. Because at heart he did have a poetic impulse, he could never sink to the extremes of certain of his contemporaries; yet his work became hard to distinguish from that of scores who called themselves "modernists." As such, he has received a measured recognition, has obtained publication in some widely circulated magazines, has won several substantial prizes, and now and then is invited to give paid readings of his poems before college groups and ladies' societies.

But Joe, the devoted poet with the faraway glitter in his eyes, is no more. Nowadays, when I come upon some published piece of his work and observe the jagged, disordered lines, I sigh to think of his onetime fervor, and of the moving lines of the earlier poems which he has disowned.

But let us go on to a second case, that of a poet whom we may know as Jack. He was of a more impulsive, energetic type than Joe, and he showed considerable ability in his smooth, imaginative lyrics. Unlike Joe, he wrote prose as well as verse—prose given to the defense and propagation of classical poetry. As editor of a small magazine, he attacked and invited his contributors to attack the extremist tendencies of the day; I can recall a letter I once received, in which he almost begged me to join him and some others in establishing a national movement for clear, sane poetry.

All this has point, however, only in view of Jack's later activities. Some of the circumstances have never been quite clear to me, although I think that a major factor was his intimate acquaintance with a certain little-known modernistic poet. In any case, I knew that he was no longer the old Jack when suddenly, without previous warning, he changed the name and character of his magazine, which proclaimed a "liberal" policy that threw it open to "poetry of every variety." This in practice meant that it began publishing the very sort of trash which its editor had previously denounced. Likewise, some examples of Jack's own work, which I have recently seen in avant-garde publications, are in no way less bizarre than the pieces he once crusaded against. It may be that in his new role as a rene-gade he is sincere, though it is hard for me to believe in his swift and total conversion. But if he expected that the transformation would provide him with a springboard to riches or fame, he mis-calculated. Today, as in the past, his work has but little vogue, pos-sibly because so many others have tried to thrust their way to recog-nition over the same gangplank. But he has lost the stanchest of his onetime friends and supporters.

Now let us glance at a final poet, whom we may call Jerry. He is a quiet, introspective man, who has written verse ever since he was in knee-pants. His production has not been voluminous, but over a period of four decades it has never ceased. During all this time, Jerry has had his eyes on quality; he has revised meticulously; he has given hours to perfecting a single line or even to the choice of a word. The result has been some exquisitely carved poems, rhythmically impeccable and stylistically flawless. Nevertheless, all Jerry's efforts may seem wasted, for he remains unknown except to a minor circle; his poems, so far as I am aware, have never been printed except in a few "little magazines" and in two small privately issued books.

Yet he goes his way undeterred, polishing his poems as pains-takingly as ever and making no concessions to the demands of the cultists—demands which, he assures me, call for work that would give him no satisfaction. "Suppose that I switched course, followed a lead that I can't respect, and wrote poems that in my heart I knew to be inferior?" he once said to me. "Even suppose that the wildly im-probable happened and I won honors and wealth—what would it all mean to me if I could no longer face myself in the mirror?"

You may say that Jerry is not being practical; you may call him a quixotic idealist. But he is such as he is, and there are not too many like him. The point, however, is that he is what he is because of his character, which has determined not his poetic ability but his poetic choices. In the same way, also, the character of Joe and of Jack has decided their poetic route. If these two had been like Jerry, they would have continued to write according to their original lights, prepared, if need be, to fight their way forward with stooped backs and bleeding fingers rather than forsake their chosen course. On the other hand, if Jerry had been like Joe or Jack, he would have swerved, twisted, compromised, and betrayed his associates and his standards, all with the object of being in the current mode and of "getting ahead." This does not necessarily mean that he would have gone far—among the shifters and machinators whom I have known, a considerable number have resembled Jack in surrendering their principles without gaining the expected rewards. In any event, Jerry would no longer be the man his friends know today. And some accomplished poems, which deserve a place in the literature of our times, would never have seen paper.

Joe, Jack, and Jerry, of course, are but representative of many who at one time or another have crossed my path. I can go back to a certain man, of real if limited ability, who wrote passable sonnets and rhymed lyrics when he came under the scrutiny of a traditional poet of his acquaintance, but would turn out incoherent, disintegrated verses as soon as his immediate mentor was a poetic "radical." I can recall a young woman, of considerable personal charm, whose gaze was so fastened on poetic awards that she almost lived from prize to prize, slanting her work to win the coveted recognitions and virtually vanishing from the poetic world when prizes ceased coming her way. I think of a certain man, whom I never met face to face and who wrote me repeatedly from prison in an eastern state (having been confined, I was told by a mutual acquaintance, for passing forged checks while under the influence of alcohol); and it comes back to me how assiduously he tried, not without ability, to perfect the sonnets which he turned out in considerable quantities under the most trying conditions. I remember another man, who wrote to me from a midwestern prison, enclosing several poignant poems which I published in my magazine *Wings;* then, after a silence of twenty-five years, wrote me again from the same penitentiary, sending some new poems and saying that he had been writing unheard during all the interval. I have recollections of the cultured middle-aged woman whom I once met for a few minutes at a poetry gathering, and who

151

later wrote me from a mental hospital, enclosing poems written with classical control on classical subjects—poems which she was producing as energetically as if the barred doors did not restrain her. My mind envisages another, a robust-looking young man pecking away at a typewriter in the office of a small western poetry magazine; and it comes back to me how, eighteen or twenty years ago, two promising successive books of his verse were issued with considerable fanfare by a major publisher . . . until, after the second book had been badly rapped by the critics, the author withdrew from the public gaze and has never since, to my knowledge, been published anywhere.

In all these cases, and in many others, including that of some elderly writers and lovers of verse who have unostentatiously served the cause of poets and poetry, the single greatest determinant of the poet's course has been the character of the poet himself. And this, I think, has been true throughout the history of poetry. Often we have direct, detailed evidence, while sometimes, as with Shakespeare, the very volume and sustained quality of a man's work testify to the pertinacity of his character. We know how the stern, strong-principled character of Milton underlay his writing, and how the studious, retiring character of Gray formed the background to his odes and his famous "Elegy," and how Wordsworth dedicated his life to the cause of poetry and never swerved from his path. In Shelley we see how a soaring lyricism arose from the character of a flamingly sensitive, sensuous, and passionate if erratic idealist. In Byron we observe a hurt, cynical, world-weary man, yet one lapped by heroic currents, so that his work ranged from fervid romanticism to the disillusioned, sardonic "Don Juan." In Emerson we find the character of a thinker, whose work reflected his inclination to enter the highlands of the mind more easily than into the typical poetic effervescences. And in Tennyson we once more have the character of one consecrated to poetry and not to be diverted by obstacles.

Few poets, indeed, ever underwent a severer test of character than Tennyson, after the critics had dealt heavy, largely unmerited blows at the *Poems* which, issued in late 1832, contained some of his best work. Beneath such discouragement, some poets would have retired from the field, in favor of a less controversial vocation such as accounting or teaching; others would have asserted themselves and defiantly done battle with their detractors. Tennyson did neither, though he did show a defeatist tendency when, in his sensitiveness to criticism, he refused the urgings of his friends to undertake further publication. However, he neither abandoned his native land nor forsook poetry. For ten years he brooded in seclusion, revising the abused poems and writing others; and when at last he emerged from his hiding place, it was with a sheaf of poems that would take a permanent place in literature.

Character, on the other hand, often had a negative influence upon poetry. We remember how Poe's unearthly talent was cramped and limited by his drinking bouts—surely he, the least prolific of our major poets, might have given us more of his marvelous songs except for this dreadful handicap. Likewise, the excesses of Baudelaire's life —the liaisons, the drugs, the alcoholism—evidently left their repercussions upon his poetry. And Coleridge might have been more productive had it not been for the tragic opium habit, which, even if it added to the color and uncanny strangeness of his verses, thereby but offers another proof of the interconnection between a poet's life and his work.

2

Thus in large part the poet's attainment is determined by factors aside from his ability and training—by the thoughts that guide him, the principles that rule him, his integrity or want of it, his strength in a crisis or his weakness before temptation. Let us suppose, for example, that you are a poet and have been taught to see poetry in lines such as Marlowe's

> Was this the face that launch'd a thousand ships
> And burnt the topless towers of Ilium?

and in passages such as Shakespeare's

Sit, Jessica: Look, how the floor of heaven
Is thick inlaid with patines of bright gold:
There's not the smallest orb which thou behold'st
But in his motion like an angel sings.

But suppose that you have a follow-the-leader disposition which makes you shiver at the very idea of pitting your own reason against the pronouncements of authority. And suppose that you are told to see poetry, let us say, in an utterance such as David Wright's in Brinnin and Read's anthology, *The Modern Poets:*

> David John Murray Wright, 6'2", myopic blue eyes . . .
> Academic achievements: B.A., Oxon (2nd class).

Or suppose that you are asked to admire a selection such as Michael McClure has contributed to the compilation *A Controversy of Poets:*

> *The Aelf-scin, The Shining Scimmer The Gleam, The Shining*
> color of walls of scratches of cracks of brightness
> the cold mystery the (Philip calls it) Weir. The déjà
> vu of the forest-sorrel, tiny, leaves sun-folded
> bent like a head in uniqueness. Animal in look
> to fold so. The moment I
> leave what I am in aelf-scin. Stand
> in wonder. Lose myself. Even to fear.
> A difference. Aelf-scin, Weir.

You might not really believe that we have here anything of the same family or order of expression as Burns' lyric that opens

> O were my love yon lilac fair,
> Wi' purple blossoms to the spring,
> And I, a bird to shelter there,
> When wearied on my little wing . . .

Or, to take an example from a less-known source, you might be unable to see any competition with this sonnet on his deceased wife

by Frederick Goddard Tuckerman (1821–73), an American poet
rescued from oblivion fifty-eight years after his death when in 1931
a selection of his poems was edited by Witter Bynner:

> One still dark night, I sat alone and wrote:
> So still it was, that distant Chanticleer
> Seemed to cry out his warning at my ear,—
> Save for the brooding echo in his throat.
> Sullen I sat; when, like the night-wind's note,
> A voice said, "Wherefore doth he weep and fear?
> Doth he not know no cry to God is dumb?"
> Another spoke: "His heart is dimmed and drowned
> With grief." I knew the shape that bended then
> To kiss me, when suddenly I once again,
> Across the watches of the starless gloom,
> Heard the cock scream and pause; the morning bell,
> Into the gulfs of Night dropped One; the vision fell,—
> And left me listening to the sinking sound.

Whatever your private reservations as to the comparative merits
of this work and that of the cold-as-stone, nose-to-earth school, you
would let your questionings remain secret. In fact, you would try
to hide them even from yourself. "Surely," you would reflect, "I
must be wrong. When so many voices are against me, how could I
possibly be right?" However, the difficulty would not lie entirely in
your lack of self-confidence. There would be a deeper compulsion:
even if you expressed a correct judgment in the face of general disagreement, that would isolate you, would leave you to follow a lone
road. And to those of us who like to travel with the crowd—which
is to say, the great majority—nothing could be more terrifying.

Therefore, with a sort of self-defensive reaction, you would tell
yourself that there must be poetry in work such as David Wright's
and Michael McClure's and in the reams of other creations on
exactly the same plane. Not for a moment could you let yourself
doubt that there was poetry in all this, although you would scrupulously avoid explaining to yourself or to anyone else just wherein the

poetry consisted. As the culminating move, in order to prove to yourself and others the absoluteness of your conformity, you would do your best to turn out poems of your own in the approved manner. This you would not find too difficult; and if in the end you won praise or even prizes, you would be doubly persuaded that now at last you were on the right track. What then, if your product was as prosy-sounding as, let us say, Wallace Stevens' "Opusculum paedagogum/The pears are not viols,/Nudes or bottles"? What if your verse were as freakish in appearance and content as the following lines by Sue Abbott Boyd in the poetry magazine *Dust*?

> Rise away and I will runsunspun
>)as you rise O . . .

Crushing down any voices of dissent lingering in your deeper self, you might be certain that you were writing poetry, and would bitterly resent any imputations to the contrary.

This is not to say that many poets of the new school do not have a deep original conviction that they are writing poetry, the *only* poetry. It could hardly be otherwise in view of the training that the young are receiving. Taught to revere the example of Eliot and Pound; taught to suppose that poetry in this century, in abandoning its foundations, has taken a prodigious leap forward, our youth can hardly be expected to have the background or the independence of mind to oppose the views being drilled into them. And so when they see, for example, that William Carlos Williams, at one place in his magnum opus, *Paterson,* has lines at odd slants, almost impossible to reproduce upon a typewriter, some of them tilted upward and some downward, with two "ands" stuck out at different angles and a quotation in French, along with one slanted line plastered in the middle, what is the poetic novice to believe? He concludes, naturally, that this is poetry, for has he not heard Williams extolled almost as a classic? And not only is it poetry but it is the latest in poetry—and the man who is unsure of himself and does not wish to be thought backward or out-of-date will, of course, be interested only in the latest poetic fads and fashions.

No doubt a person of rare judgment and strong independent will would decide that there was something wrong here; he might even conclude that if the currently recommended work is poetry, then he would rather turn to stockbroking. But the person of rare judgment and strong independent will is certain to be much in the minority. In the rank and file of young poets, man's natural sheep-follow-sheep disposition will assert itself. Hence it is not to the great majority of writers but to the determined leaders that we must look for a reversal of present disruptive trends. Only by the character of the leaders—their strength, their courage, their assertiveness in separating true products from counterfeit and genuine principles from pretense and illusion—can poetry in our age be saved.

XII

CRITICS UNDER A CLOUD

I

Some years ago two Australian soldiers, Lieutenant James MacAuley and Corporal Harold Stewart, decided to test the insight of modern critics of poetry. Having an afternoon to spare, they picked words and phrases from various books at random and wove them into meaningless phrases, their only principle being that they must have no principle. That is to say, they scrupulously avoided any coherent theme, while contenting themselves "with confused and inconsistent hints at the meaning." The first three lines of one "poem," for example, were lifted from a report on the drainage of the breeding places of mosquitoes. It was not enough, however, for the enterprising MacAuley and Stewart to invent poems; they must also create a poet. This they did with an air of great discovery; and thus the mythical Ern Malley came into being, and was even supplied with a biography, including details of the disease from which he allegedly died.

Doubtless all this provided something of a lark for MacAuley and Stewart. And yet Ern Malley and his poems were taken seriously. The Australian literary review *Angry Penguins* hailed him as "one of the giants," one who "worked from disciplined and restrained statements into the deepest wells of human experience." Thirty pages of one issue were devoted to the find, while elsewhere too his work was acclaimed, as in an American publication that found it to possess "a richness and breadth of vocabulary that is quite amazing. . . . Everything is there in such a creative form that the uncommunicable is communicated."

Now let us observe just how Malley "communicated the uncommunicable." Here, for example, are some lines from "Documentary Film," chosen by Harry Roskelenko and Elizabeth Lambert for a magazine selection of Australian verse:

> There have been interpolations, false-syndromes
> Like a rivet through the hand
> Such deliberate suppressions of crisis as
> Footscray.

Footscray, it should be explained, is a malodorous Melbourne suburb.

This also is from "Documentary Film":

> Innumerable the images
> The register of birth and dying
> Under the carved rococo porch
> The Tigris—Venice—Melbourne—the Ch'en Plain—
> And the sound track like a trail of saliva.

Now consider this passage:

> Eructation of unhealthy souls
> Into the faded air, the torpid
> Driven into the wind that sweeps the gloomy hills of London,
> Hamstead and Clerkenwell, Campden and Putney,
> Highgate, Primrose and Ludgate. Not here
> Not here the darkness, in this twittering world.

I will admit that the latter, from T. S. Eliot's *Four Quartets,* contains nothing quite so bad as the concluding line of the first selection, and I make no suggestion that it was intended as a hoax. But if it is not of the same genus and species of writing, then a camel is a wholly different kind of animal from a dromedary.

But to return to Ern Malley. "Documentary Film" proceeds:

> The slant sun now descending
> Upon the montage of the desecrate womb
> Opened like a drain.
> The young men aspire
> Like departing souls from leaky roofs
> And fractured imploring windows too.
> All must be synchronized the jagged
> Quartz of vision with the asphalt of human speech.

Pretty bad, isn't it? In fact, now that the hoax has been exposed, who would deny that it is senseless, ludicrous, grossly unpoetic? Yet in the pages of one of the best and most respected American literary magazines, a critic spoke of Malley's "beautifully integrated body of erudition" and of his "purity of vision." But stop! Let us not strike too harsh a blow at the poor ghost of Ern Malley! After all, is his work really inferior to much that has been acclaimed time after time—such work as we have noted in these pages from writers well-known and little-known?

Even if the Malley case stood alone, it would be revealing—not so much in indicating the prevalence of hoaxes as in proving the incapacity of some of our critics to distinguish between the true and the false and their consequent inability to perform their all-important duties as watchdogs at the gates of poetry. Unfortunately, however, the Malley case does not stand alone. Many years before, when the free verse movement in America was in its early stages, the poets Witter Bynner and Arthur Davison Ficke joined forces in originating the "Spectric" school of poets—a school that had no more real existence than Ern Malley was to have. Mr. Bynner, as reported by Howard Willard Cook in *Our Poets of Today*, has explained how he found his inspiration:

> Imagists and Vorticists long had aroused my ire, and one
> day in Chicago I determined to form an ultra-modern school

of poetry myself just to show how easily it might be done. I was attending a performance of the Russian Ballet in Chicago at the moment when the idea struck me. What should I call my new school? I looked down at my program and found it opened at "Le Spectre de la Rose." The word spectre struck me. Spectrists—that was a good, suggestive name. I adopted it forthwith.

Mr. Bynner's collaborator, Arthur Davison Ficke, expounded the meaning of "Spectric" in his preface to their joint effort, *Spectra, A Book of Poetic Experiments:*

In the first place, it speaks, to the mind, of that process of diffraction by which are disarticulated the several colored and other rays of which light is composed. It indicates our feeling that the theme of a poem is to be regarded as a prism upon which the colorless white light of infinite existence falls and is broken up into glowing, beautiful, and intelligible hues. . . . These specters are the manifold spells and the true essence of objects—like the magic that would inevitably encircle a mirror from the hand of Helen of Troy.

As an example of the "Spectric" poems, here are some lines from Opus 195 by Anne Knish (Arthur Davison Ficke):

> Her soul was freckled
> Like the bald head
> Of a jaundiced Jewish banker.
> Her fair and featurous face
> Writhed like
> An albino boa-constrictor. . . .

And here is an excerpt from Opus 63, by Emmanuel Morgan (Witter Bynner), who wrote in rhyme, whereas his collaborator dispensed with rhyme:

> A simian shape
> Throwing seven souls on the sea-wet cape;
> Even for us

Who smile mouth to mouth,
The full tornado from the seven-forked south;
Even to us
Who clasp with our knees,
The scattering upheaval of the seven cold seas!

The reactions to the "Spectric" poems were much like the reactions in a later day to Ern Malley. Ficke's high-sounding introductory bombast was taken seriously, and so were the supposed poems. Published under a respected imprint, they were widely praised (that is, until the hoaxers revealed the trick, after which most of the critics reversed themselves).

As recently as 1965, attention has been attracted to the case of Hugh MacDiarmid, whose real name is Christopher Murray Grieve. A discussion in the *Literary Supplement* of the London *Times,* as reported by Anthony Lewis in *The New York Times Book Review,* revolved about the question "whether a poet was breaking the rules if he took another man's prose, rearranged the lines in verse form and published the result as his own." In other words, was plagiarism permissible?

The dispute began with a poem by MacDiarmid entitled "Perfect," which an anonymous reviewer in the *Literary Supplement* praised as "a small imagist masterpiece," and which was described in a book by Professor Kenneth Buthlay as "the poem that Ezra Pound and the Imagists talked about but did not write." This poem began as follows:

I found a pigeon's skull on the machair.
All the bones pure white and dry, and chalky,
But perfect,
Without a crack or a flaw anywhere.

This, of course, is no better or worse than thousands of compositions offered nowadays as poetry; it is not extreme, it is merely straight prose. In this case, however, proof that it was straight prose was contained in a letter to the *Literary Supplement* by Glyn Jones of Wales, who revealed that a short story of his, published in 1937, had contained all the lines of the alleged poem except the first. To be sure, the short story had not been printed with the broken appearance of verse.

In other instances also, MacDiarmid was shown to have taken singular liberties, as was disclosed when the correspondent Hugh Gordon Porteus made it known that Mr. Jones was "not the only writer to have the honor of seeing his prose, without so much as a by-your-leave, transmuted into the splendid poetry of Mr. Hugh MacDiarmid."

Further revelations followed, such as that "the poet, in a work on the German writer Karl Kraus, had lifted 139 lines intact from a review of a Kraus book in the *Times Literary Supplement* itself. . . . Do your reviewers perhaps write in verse?" asked the correspondent. "And if so, are the poems not copyright?"

For our purposes, obviously, the point of all this is not that one modernist poet was caught, and caught repeatedly, in the act of cheating. This in itself says nothing against the movement; a traditional poet might equally be found to be cheating, and some have indeed been detected in acts of plagiarism. But what is of real concern is the extent to which the critics were hoodwinked by the stolen prose which MacDiarmid rearranged and reprinted as poetry. His work, which has appeared in many anthologies, including his own *The Golden Treasury of Scottish Poetry,* has been described by Babette Deutsch in her *Poetry in Our Time* as showing "a ranging, aggressive mind"; in fact, he is "the leader of the Scotch renaissance." Selden Rodman, in the Appendix to *A New Anthology of Modern Poetry,* tells us that "he has been compared to Robert Burns." And M. L. Rosenthal, who devotes four pages to the Scottish writer in *The Modern Poets,* remarks that "MacDiarmid is probably the least known of poets in our language who might conceivably be called 'great.'"

I wish you hadn't
caught that cold, but the dead we miss are easier
to talk to: with those no longer
tensed by problems one cannot feel shy and, anyway,
when playing cards or drinking
or pulling faces are out of the question, what else is there
to do but talk to the voices
of conscience they have become?

This excerpt from W. H. Auden is not quoted because, as modern verse goes, it is either strikingly good or arrestingly bad. It is cited not for itself at all but as an illustration of the sort of work that evokes critical enthusiasm nowadays. These lines, writes Frank W. Warnke in *The New Republic,* are from a "moving elegy" and indicate "the superficially relaxed but subtly masterful technique" of Auden's volume *About the House.* In making this appraisal, the reviewer goes no further than is usual among modern critics and is more restrained than many. Yet note the implications of his remarks.

First, as to the "masterful technique"—"I wish you hadn't caught that cold, but the dead we miss are easier to talk to"—if this represents "masterful" poetic technique or any technique at all, then I must commend the poetic technique of the first sentence my eyes chance to encounter in the first book I pull at random out of the shelves, which happens to be *The Diary of Søren Kierkegaard:* "I can't bother to do anything whatsoever; I can't bother to walk—the effort is too great." These lines, which you would hardly acclaim even as distinguished prose, were manifestly not regarded by their author as poetic, and even less as "masterly" in technique. They are, of course, of the same breed of prose as the Auden excerpt, the main difference being that they are printed as prose. But the point most worth noting is that the moderns, having abandoned technique in the name of "freedom," are lauded by the critics for their use of the very instrument they have relinquished. They are, literally, allowed to eat their cake and have it too.

At the same time, they are applauded for other qualities which they possess only as a mole possesses wings. For example, the critic Glauco Cambon speaks of the "lyrical statement" in the lines of William Carlos Williams ending:

> Compose. (No ideas
> but in things.) Invent!
> Saxifrage is my flower that splits
> the rocks.

And the same tendency to give unearned credit is illustrated by Frank J. Warnke's reference to Auden's "moving elegy." The lines, written in memory of Louis MacNeice, are clearly elegiac in theme —but if that is enough to create a "moving elegy," then every obituary notice in the newspapers is an elegy. Here again the critic fails to recognize the nature of poetry. He seems not to understand that the mere statement of fact does not make poetry; it takes much more, including feeling, music, imagination, along with suggestions of realities deeper than the words themselves. There is nothing elegiac because there is nothing poetic in lines like the following (to offer a further excerpt commended by Mr. Warnke):

> dear Shade, for your elegy
> I should have been able to manage
> something more like you than this egocentric monologue,
> but accept it for friendship's sake.

The spirit of the elegy is to be found in a stanza like this from Matthew Arnold's "Requiescat":

> Strew on her roses, roses,
> And never a spray of yew.
> In quiet she reposes:
> Ah! would that I did too.

The spirit of the elegy is evident in "The Tryst," by the twentieth-century British poet E. V. Rieu, as this stanza will indicate:

Joy as of old in her melodious moods,
Who is made one with universal things,
Will be his stay. And if to him she brings
Her human sorrow in the rain, and broods
Over the autumn magic of the woods,
In such full griefs there is no room for pain,
But wonder and the touch of peace again,
And trysting in the haunted solitudes.

In these selections the authors say more than would be possible in prose, and say it more concisely, effectively, and memorably. The distinction between offerings such as Auden's and the lyrics by Arnold and Rieu needs to be recognized not only by the poets but by the critics if pseudopoetry is not to obliterate the genuine. In generally overlooking such a distinction, the critics have made it possible not only for nontechnique to be applauded as masterly technique but for prose to be touted as poetry in areas calling for the utmost in lyrical grace, delicacy, and perceptiveness.

3

In most fields of activity an object cannot be at once long and short, hot and cold, round and square, or all-white and all-black. Such limitations, however, do not apply in the criticism of modern poetry. Here, in a sort of "Alice in Wonderland" miracle world, the laws of nature are suspended—one might almost say, transcended. We have seen an example in the "masterful technique" of work that had forsaken technique. And other cases are not hard to find. Thus Charles Olson, in his "statement on poetics" in Donald M. Allen's *The New American Poetry,* can solemnly announce that listening for the syllables of poetry "must be so constant and so scrupulous, the exaction must be so complete, that the assurance of the ear is purchased at the highest—40 hours a day—price." And the English poet Stephen Spender, in an article, "Can't We Do Without the Poets," contributed some years ago to *The New York Times Book*

Review, speaks of "the serious non-seriousness of poetry," in which "the form is non-serious in the way that a game such as a crossword puzzle is," while "the precision of logic or science is brought to bear just as much on the non-serious as on the serious element."

Leaving it for the reader to decide how this deft trick can be accomplished, and how the form of poetry can be legitimately compared to that of a crossword puzzle, let us go on to a statement of Spender's in his book *The Struggle of the Modern:*

> Surrealism adopts non-literary techniques in order to stimulate a stream of images, coming, supposedly, from the subconscious mind. The surrealists wished to break down the boundaries of literature altogether, and make poetry a machinery for drilling through the surface of consciousness into the world of passions and fantasies below. Surrealism was the attempt to liberate among the sane the forces of insanity . . .

Now I do not challenge the accuracy of this diagnosis. In fact, I regard it as distinctly helpful in appraising the part that not only surrealistic poets but surrealistic critics of poetry have been playing, and in attempting to understand their evident dexterity in reconciling irreconcilables.

Not that such dexterity need be related to surrealism. More often it represents merely a confused attempt to find a logical basis for illogical and contradictory procedures. This is the sort of dexterity displayed by John Holmes when, in Don Cameron Allen's compilation *The Moment of Poetry,* he refers to Harriet Monroe, first editor and founder of *Poetry, A Magazine of Verse,* as a "good hostess who printed, I am sure, poems she did not like and could not really understand . . . because she respected them." And similar dexterity is exhibited by David Daiches in his book of *Literary Essays.* After quoting one of the offerings of Dylan Thomas, he remarks, "There is no obscurity here," and proceeds to explain away the obscurity.

On the same page, referring to Thomas' extraordinary phrase, "the synagogue of the ear of corn" (which almost seems to convert the ear of corn to Judaism), Daiches points out that "synagogue . . . has no meaning but the literal one, and therefore can be used freshly in a non-literal way," which is like saying that green has no meaning but green, and therefore can be used to designate purple. And on the next page, Daiches justifies Thomas' use of "long friends" to imply worms: "worms for Thomas were not disgusting, but profoundly symbolic: like maggots they are elements of corruption and thus of reunification, of eternity." To anyone who has ever seen the hideous sight of maggots squirming and swarming, this will seem curious information.

Next turn to C. M. Bowra's scholarly book, *The Creative Experiment.* Here again we have an effort to harmonize fire and water; this is evident when the critic quotes from T. S. Eliot:

If you don't like it you can get on with it, I said,
Others can pick and choose if you can't.

This, declares Mr. Bowra, "does create a peculiar kind of poetry. . . . The dull, trite words ring so true that they achieve the effect of drama, and their succinct, practical air has its own attraction."

This is the more confusing since "dull, trite words" are precisely what most exponents of the new movement claim to be revolting against. But the commentator is the victim of no small-minded consistency. Moreover, he does not bother to note that an "effect of drama"—even if these blank, prosy lines really do have a dramatic impact—is not necessarily related to poetry. And even if a "succinct, practical air has its own attraction," what has such an attraction to do with poetry? The words "Dinner is ready" or "Here is the check we owe you" also have a succinct, practical air.

But this is merely one more illustration of the way in which some critics twist language and logic in their effort to bridge the gulf between modern verse and poetry.

Other critics, meanwhile, proceed by means of half-truths, false analogies, and pontifical statements of negligible content. Testimony to this fact may be seen in *The Background of Modern Poetry*, by J. Isaacs, in which we are told:

> There is pure poetry and there is impure poetry, social and political poetry. In texture modern poetry is a poetry of nuances. In structure it is a balance of tensions and conflicts. At its worst it is a cluster of disorganized and incoherent fragments; at its best it is a dome of many-colored glass, staining the white radiance of eternity.

This sounds imposing, doesn't it? But look at Mr. Isaacs' remarks a little more closely. The first statement is a truism, which, with a change or two in wording, might equally pertain to peanut butter or soap. The second sentence is meaningless unless explained—what is there about "a poetry of nuances" that was beyond the range of Shakespeare, Milton, and Keats? The remark about "a balance of tensions and conflicts" might fittingly apply to the Cold War or to the relations of capital and labor. And the statement about "a cluster of disorganized and incoherent fragments" might refer to a bombed city. As for the concluding phrase, with its quotation (without quotes) from Shelley, it fits the rest of the passage about like a jeweled lid clamped down on a cabbage pot.

The writer is typically in the modern vein in a further passage such as

> Poetry is made up of comparisons, simple or complex, open or concealed. The richness of poetry is obtained by mixing or interweaving or juxtaposing these comparisons. The mixture is either a mechanical mixture or a chemical mixture: when the mechanical becomes chemical the explosion takes place.

This, to my mind, sounds suspiciously like the language used by Arthur Davison Ficke in expounding his Spectric hoax. I am left wondering just how "the mechanical becomes chemical" and just what a "chemical mixture" in poetry may be.

Nevertheless, the criticism of men like Isaacs, Bowra, and Daiches is almost conservative beside some modern commentary. When the critics must explain something really difficult—for example, the verbal acrobatics, the fragmentation of words, and the fantastic punctuation of E. E. Cummings—we can look for great resourcefulness in analysis. A case in point is that of M. L. Rosenthal in *The Modern Poets, A Critical Introduction*. One would know this from Mr. Rosenthal's remark that "Cummings' great forte is the manipulation of traditional forms and attitudes in an original way." Without trying to puzzle out how the flouter of tradition has come to manipulate traditional forms and attitudes "in an original way," let us go on to some of Mr. Rosenthal's further findings:

> Every unorthodoxy of punctuation, spacing, and noncapitalization . . . in Cummings' poems generally, can be read functionally. . . . The unclosed parenthesis, for instance, walls off what has gone before just enough so that the wondering, rather chilled awe of the poem's final moment is given tremendous emphasis, and the absence of a period suggests that this last effect is of a realization that must continue without a stop. . . . Some of the poems, for instance, the grasshopper poem in *no thanks* which begins "r-p-o-p-h-e-s-s-a-g-r" and rises to the first climax of "PPEGORHASS" and the second of ".gRrEaPsPhOs" *cannot* be read aloud at these key points The whole life, and joke, of the poem consists in a pictorially kinetic effect typographically created to represent the insect bunching itself up to leap—distorting itself and scattering itself about in the sense that its normal appearance in repose is scrambled during its various movements—and then coming to rest rearranged, or, as Cummings shows it,
>
> to
> rea(be)rran(com)gi(e)ngly
> ,grasshopper;
>
> . . . The poem is a kind of mechanical toy, but an ingenious one that works.

Let us consider some further criticism in the same general vein. The commentator is analyzing a piece entitled "Forest Fire," which he quotes:

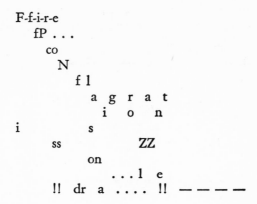

"One stands breathless," writes the critic, "before such consummate command of form over content. Here poetry is lifted to a new elevation. One cannot admire too strongly the deftness and restraint with which the poet develops his theme to a crescendo, beginning with his evocative statement of elementary fact, then subtly suggesting the spread of the fire by the widening spaces between the letters of the craftily chosen key word 'conflagration,' which is necessarily presented in a disordered form to indicate the confusion and terror of the catastrophe. In the consummate concluding lines, in which a lesser artist might have impaired the effect by more specific statement, we have a typographically created impression of chaos, suggested by a broken word such as 'hiss' and by the skillfully misplaced letters and punctuation marks, all of which add eloquently to the complex simplicity and the dissociated unity of the whole."

Now this commentary, I submit, is typical of the modern vein, as represented by critics of the school of M. L. Rosenthal. Then do these words express a profound insight, a penetrating analysis of an able poem? Not at all! I myself, without the ghostliest attempt at poetic accomplishment, composed "Forest Fire" almost as fast as I could hit the typewriter keys, and immediately afterward wrote the pretended criticism in the full consciousness that the lines enjoyed no such merits as I asserted.

But let us go on to other phases of modern criticism.

XIII

FREEDOM THROUGH DICTATORSHIP

I

The man who clamps down chains in the name of liberation has become proverbial. No one is a more ardent advocate of freedom—but his idea of freedom is something that does not tie his own hands. If, for example, he seeks religious liberty, he will grant the followers of all faiths the opportunity to believe exactly as he does, in the way of the Puritans who came to New England in pursuit of the right to worship as they saw fit, then persecuted Roger Williams, Anne Hutchinson, and other dissidents for worshipping as *they* saw fit.

But in the arts we would look for such repressiveness less than in any other field. In the arts we would expect the true liberalism that permits each man to obey the prompting within him. It is therefore a sad reflection that the arts have not been immune to intolerance—the intolerance that masks suppression and even tyranny beneath the name of freedom. And an especially unhappy fact is that, of all the arts, none have been worse afflicted than poetry.

I might go to the extent of saying that, more and more, observing the outpourings of modernistic critics of poetry, I have noticed how religiously they have toed the Party Line. Not that they are Communists or Fascists—merely that they have established a Party Line of their own, and obey techniques like those of the totalitarians in their efforts to extirpate all opposition. Just as faithful Marxists hurl gibes and insults at the "decadent capitalists" and "petty bourgeois," so the True Believers of the new literary cults take pleasure in smearing the names, the accomplishments, the very minds and spirits of poets so unworthy as to have lived before Eliot and to have written in a non-Eliot tradition. It follows, of course, that they refuse to tolerate writers who depart so far from the Party Line as to see merit in the earlier tradition.

In his book *What Is Poetry?*, John Hall Wheelock has pointedly expressed the situation:

> . . . in our time, any deviation in the arts from the taste prescribed must face criticism that is not aesthetic judgment so much as moral condemnation. The heretic is burned at the stake.

Among the many instances of such fanaticism, one of the clearest I have recently seen is provided by F. R. Leavis in his paperback, *New Bearings in English Poetry*. This book, issued by a great university press, is marked by such intellectual snobbishness, such presumptions and such condescension that it would not be worth mentioning did it not perfectly illustrate a type—a type that has become increasingly common, particularly in our institutions of learning. Like all critics of his school, Mr. Leavis dutifully approves what he is expected to approve: Eliot, Pound, and Hopkins; and he lashes out with innuendoes and blanket condemnations against poets proscribed by the Party.

Perhaps the least of his offenses is to refer to that writer of exquisite verse, Arthur O'Shaughnessy, as a "poetaster." He disposes of Masefield (whom he does not even mention by name) by linking him with that other superb poet, James Elroy Flecker, as if this proved both to be unworthy of consideration. He refers to Andrew Lang's accomplished sonnet *The Odyssey* with a sneer as illustrating "very neatly the kind of thing that cultured people in the latter part of the nineteenth century took poetry to be." And he describes Meredith's *Modern Love* as "the flashy product of unusual but vulgar cleverness working upon cheap emotion." Admirers of Browning will be a little taken aback at this characterization: "So inferior a mind and spirit as Browning's could not provide the impulse needed to bring back into poetry the adult intelligence." Hardy is disposed of with the bland statement that his "solidity appears archaic." Rupert Brooke is annihilated with a phrase: "an inhibiting adolescent self-consciousness in an ironical disguise." And so on and on. By contrast, the reader is startled to be told in regard to that nineteenth-century modern Gerard Manley Hopkins that his imagery "and his way of using the body and movement of the language, are like Shakespeare's." The reputation of Shakespeare has survived other blows, and one assumes that it will outlive this comparison.

Doubtless, also, Browning, Hardy, Brooke, and the others will retain some measure of approval. But what shall one say of poetry in an age represented by critics who follow the Party Line with such a stern disapproving eye for deviationists and counterrevolutionaries not only present but past?

A second case may be worth noting. I have before me W. H. Auden's *A Selection from the Poems of Alfred, Lord Tennyson,* and am struck by some remarkable statements: Tennyson "had the finest ear, perhaps, of any English poet," but "he was also undoubtedly the stupidest," and "he was a fool to try to write a poetry which would teach the Ideal." A moment's thought will show the fallacy of both statements. A stupid poet would not be obsessed— as was Tennyson, according to Auden's own acknowledgment— by the twin questions, "Who am I? Why do I exist?" Nor could a stupid poet erect the magnificent lifelong edifice that is our heritage from the Victorian Poet Laureate. As for teaching the Ideal: Tennyson tries not so much to teach as to express the Ideal, which is something different entirely. But in making his charge, Auden is true to the Party Line, since any thought of the Ideal is anathema to the modern poet, much as the thought of God is an impiety to the true-believing Marxist. In accusing Tennyson of preeminent stupidity, Auden again toes the Party Line, which requires a general downgrading of yesterday's poets, especially those whose standards were furthest from those of our own revolutionaries. This does not necessarily mean, of course, that Auden was conscious of toeing the Party Line, nor that there may not be just reasons for deprecating the work even of outstanding past poets. But the Party precepts and disciplines have become so deeply instilled into the modernistic critic that he conforms to them almost automatically.

Another example is provided by Allen Tate in his book of critical essays, *On the Limits of Poetry*. What disturbs me here is not that the author exercises the critic's legitimate right to object to any literary work, no matter how celebrated. What disturbs me is the pontifical assumption and the dry rationalistic analysis with which, like so many of the "advanced" critics, he disposes of the romantics. Take his attitude to Shelley's famous lines:

> Life, like a dome of many-colored glass,
> Stains the white radiance of eternity.

"As a product of the imagination," Mr. Tate remarks, "this passage is incomprehensible; as a practical, that is to say, a scientific generalization, it is open to the just contempt of the scientific mind."

Now why, one may ask, should these lines be regarded as a "practical" or a "scientific generalization"? Does the critic draw no distinction between practicality and science, on the one hand, and poetry, on the other? Is he under the illusion that he is reviewing a textbook on optics? If so, it is not hard to see why the lines should be incomprehensible—incomprehensible to him, although not to the generations of readers who have found them to be illuminated with magnificence and meaning. If the enemies of poetry wish to diminish the art, there is no surer way than to reduce its utterances to "practical" and "scientific generalizations."

This method may be illustrated by an imagined instance. Suppose that a critic is examining the passage in "Lycidas" in which Milton declares that the "day-star"

Flames in the forehead of the morning sky.

"This," the commentator might proclaim, "is incomprehensible. It is subject to the just contempt of the scientific mind. The idea that an indefinite entity such as the sky should have a forehead has no authorization in experimental fact. The figure, moreover, embodies a personification that is unjustified in the practical sense. Are we to suppose that Milton conceives of the sky as a living being, and one with human qualities?"

"But this criticism," the reader will argue, "is preposterous. It wholly misses the point and spirit of a majestic line. It attempts to hold the poet down to standards which are not those of poetry, and overlooks the distinction between practicality and the poetic imagination."

The reader will, of course, be justified in these objections. And yet our imagined critic of Milton but follows the tactics of the actual critic of Shelley. By the same method, he could annihilate the brilliant metaphorical passages in Shakespeare, along with the fancies and fervors of every other poet from Pindar to Walter de la Mare. By the same method he would treat the sunset as a mere subject for spectroscopic analysis, and would study the beauty of the rose by dissecting its petals on a laboratory table.

If Mr. Tate's strictures against Shelley were isolated phenomena, they might be overlooked. Consider, however, his reactions to this stanza from Keats' "Ode to a Nightingale":

Fade far away, dissolve, and quite forget
    What thou among the leaves hast never known,
The weariness, the fever, and the fret
    Here, where men sit and hear each other groan;

Where palsy shakes a few, sad, last gray hairs,
   Where youth grows pale, and spectre-thin, and dies;
   Where but to think is to be full of sorrow
      And leaden-eyed despairs,
   Where Beauty cannot keep her lustrous eyes,
      Or new Love pine at them beyond to-morrow.

"Looked at from any point of view," Mr. Tate assures us, "this stanza is bad; the best that ought to be said of it perhaps is that there are worse things in Shelley and Wordsworth, and in Keats himself."

How does the critic justify this contemptuous sniff of dismissal? "Keats," he tells us, "has no language of his own for this form of experience. . . . To put it 'cognitively,' he lacks an ordered symbolism through which he may *know* the common and the ideal reality in a single imaginative act." I must confess that I am baffled by this analysis, particularly as I have not the least intimation of what an "ideal reality" may be. But perhaps light is thrown on this dark point by the poems that the critic does approve. In a later section of the book, he refers to the "typically modern, rootless, and internationalized intelligence" of Ezra Pound (who, incidentally, used that "internationalized intelligence" during World War II on behalf of America's enemy Mussolini). And he quotes an example of Pound's "distinguished verse":

And they want to know what we talked about? *"de litteris*
      et de armis, praestantibus ingeniis,
Both of ancient times and our own; books, arms,
And men of unusual genius
Both of ancient times and our own, in short the usual subjects
Of conversation between intelligent men."

Are we to suppose that this, with its Latin quotation followed by commonplaces in English prose, is what the critic means by "a language of his own"? Have we here "an ordered symbolism" through which a poet may know "the common and the ideal reality"? But even if we indulgently answer, "Yes!" we are left in confusion. For how explain Mr. Tate's further remarks? After stating his belief that Pound "is probably one of two or three living Americans who will be remembered as poets of the first order," he goes on to state:

> . . . There is no reason to infer from that that Mr. Pound, outside his craft (or outside his written conversation) knows in the least what he is doing or saying.

I leave it for the reader to fathom this. As for myself—I cannot help feeling just a little chilled to remember that the dictatorship which dominates present-day poetry, and which would rule out so much as a hearing for a budding Shelley or Keats, is typified by an outlook which can be so severe on the authors of "Adonais" and "Ode to a Nightingale" and so ebullient as to the creator of the "Pisan Cantos."

2

Hermann Hagedorn, a poet better known a generation ago than today, has a sonnet in which he refers to "The quiet shutting, one by one, of doors." Although this was not meant to apply to the condition of poetry, nevertheless it does describe the plight of the whole school of twentieth-century writers of traditional verse, of which Hagedorn was himself a member.

Door after door, during recent years, has been quietly shutting against these poets. They have been debarred almost entirely from the pages of the more prominent and most of the less prominent literary periodicals as well as from the organs of the so-called intelligentsia, which formerly gave them an audience; even when a rare traditionalist is tolerated, he is usually someone with the established reputation of a Hardy or a Masefield. Meanwhile the less celebrated traditionalists are overlooked in readings and discussions at poetry centers, at universities, and in sophisticated programs over FM radio stations. They are excluded from college classrooms in favor of Eliot, William Carlos Williams, Dylan Thomas, and their like.

They are scorned by the judges of prize committees, as in the recent awards of Pulitzer Prizes in poetry to Robert Lowell, Theodore Roethke, Louis Simpson, and other insurgents, and in major prizes to Pound, Cummings, Marianne Moore, and their prominent fellow "modernists." In fact, aside from the special case of Robert Frost— whom even the most fanatical innovator would find it hard to over- look—one has trouble in recalling any traditionalist at all who has been awarded any important prize in a competition supposedly open to poets of all persuasions. The unanimity has been just what one would expect of a group of Democrats voting on whether to turn the political spoils over to the Republicans, or of a caucus of Repub- licans making a similar decision as to the Democrats.

Equally one-sided, and of even greater importance, has been the situation in relation to anthologies. I say "even greater importance," since the anthologies will provide future generations with samplings of present-day work; largely by means of the anthologies, the critics of tomorrow will be enabled to choose among the poets of today. Just what, therefore, do we find in recent anthologies?

Let us consider some general compilations of American verse. To begin with the latest, I have in my hands a bulky work, *American Poetry,* edited by three college professors: Gay Wilson Allen, Wal- ter B. Rideout, and James K. Robinson. Published in January, 1966 (although bearing a 1965 copyright notice), this "full-scale anthol- ogy" includes, according to the dust jacket, "fifty of the best American poets from colonial times to the present." The earlier choices are, of course, not relevant to our discussion; but if you look over the four or five hundred pages devoted to the poets who wrote mainly or entirely in the twentieth century, you will find those two prominent traditionalists of an earlier generation, Edwin Arlington Robinson and Robert Frost. Also, you will find twenty-seven recent versifiers associated in some way with the "modern" movement, in- cluding some as well known as "e. e. cummings" and T. S. Eliot, but not excluding several still uncelebrated writers, such as James Dickey, Robert Creeley, and Denise Levertov, whose work manifests the orthodox modernist contempt for rhyme and meter and for most of what used to be considered the poetic proprieties. An example may be seen in a passage such as this, by Robert Creeley:

> The push
> > beyond and
> into
> Respect, they said he respected the
> ones with the learning, lacking it
> himself
> > (Waldo Frank & his
> 6 languages)
> > What had seemed
> important
> *While Crane sailed to Mexico I was writing*
> (so that one betrayed
> > himself)

The selection of such dissociated gabble by a writer previously unknown to fame (and, if one can judge by this nonpoetry, deservedly unknown) takes on especial point in view of what the anthologists have not selected. You could range all through this voluminous collection without realizing that American poetry had ever been graced by the work of Edwin Markham, Edna St. Vincent Millay, Vachel Lindsay, Arthur Davison Ficke, Witter Bynner, Hermann Hagedorn, John G. Neihardt, William Ellery Leonard, Stephen Vincent Benét, William Rose Benét, Robert Hillyer, George Santayana, Thomas S. Jones, Jr., Sara Teasdale, Jessie B. Rittenhouse, Anna Hemstead Branch, Elinor Wylie, Ridgely Torrence, Shaemas O'Sheel, Odell Shepard, Struthers Burt, Joseph Auslander, Leonard Bacon, Ruth Guthrie Harding, Robert Nathan, David Morton, Cale Young Rice, Lizette Woodworth Reese, George Sterling, Margaret Widdemer, Don Marquis, Arthur Guiterman, Mark van Doren, Robert P. Tristram Coffin, Daniel Whitehead Hicky, or John Hall Wheelock. This list makes no attempt at completeness; but it includes American poets of this century who achieved not only success in their work but some measure of recognition; it does not cover any of the many with whom I have come into contact and whose work is meritorious and even memorable although not widely known. Although one or two of those listed, such as Lindsay and Millay, have made appearances on both sides of the poetic fence, all did produce able, sometimes outstandingly able, work in the traditional forms; I can well remember how at one time they and their kindred seemed to be bringing America to the dawn of a great poetic renaissance.

Any particular poet on the list, to be sure, might be rejected by a legitimate exercise of the anthologists' critical judgment. But how can they *all* be ignored? How is it possible for you to thumb your way through a "full-scale" new anthology of American poetry without receiving the faintest intimation that even one of these men or women ever put a line on paper? Is there any explanation except that the anthologists, who are perhaps so indoctrinated as not to be fully aware what they are doing, are faithful treaders of the Party Line? that they select only within the narrow and dogmatic limits of their own poetic sect, and rule out all freedom of poetic creation except that which conforms to their prescribed pattern?

"Ah, yes," you may answer. "But this, after all, is only one anthology—and one anthology does not make American literature, any more than one pine tree makes a forest. Even if the editors' eyes have been fogged by prejudices or misconceptions, it does not follow that other anthologists share their bias."

This would seem to be a valid point. Let us go on, therefore, to other anthologies.

Here before me are eight additional recent compilations of American verse. Three of them, all large paperbacks, can be classed together: *The New American Poetry, 1954–1960*, edited by Donald M. Allen (1960); *Poets of Today*, edited by Walter Lowenfels (1964); and *A Controversy of Poets*, edited by Paris Leary and Robert Kelly (1965). All three lean so heavily to one side that they call for little attention. All are dominated by that conventional unconventionality which excludes every feature generally associated with poetry before about the year 1920, including rhyme and meter and almost every suggestion of an effort to rise above prose. Lines no more poetic than "On Sunday afternoon we ate a big dinner,/all fourteen of us," and "We'd liberated Naples and the Wops/had come aboard to work cargo," are to be found throughout, along with many more extreme examples, and no poet halfway as conservative as Robert Frost is included.

Claims to a greater catholicity, however, will be seen in the other five collections, none of which date back before 1955, and the first three of which are hard-cover books: Lord Cecil and Allen Tate's *Modern Verse in English;* W. H. Auden's *The Criterion Book of Modern American Verse;* Conrad Aiken's *Twentieth Century American Poetry;* Oscar Williams' *The New Pocket Anthology of American Verse;* and *The Conscious Voice, An Anthology of American Poetry from the Seventeenth Century to the Present,* compiled by Albert D. Van Nostrand and Charles H. Watts II. To set down the minutiae of each collection would be tiresome if not unrewarding; but I have examined each in detail, and some conclusions emerge.

The first and most important finding is that all five books follow the same general principles of selection, and have the same general slant. There are, of course, individual variations, but the lion's share of favor in all the collections is given to apostles of the new movement, while few followers of poetry's central tradition are admitted. Inevitably, Robinson and Frost are represented in every compilation; but aside from these two, only modernists are included among the eight poets of this century covered in *The Conscious Voice.* Perhaps still more startling is the case of *Modern Verse in English,* in which sixty-one American poets of this century are given space, but the writers in rhyme and meter number only four or five apart from the two mentioned above, and even these four or five are relatively neglected (thus, ten pages are devoted to Pound and twenty-five to Eliot as against a single page for Edna St. Vincent Millay). One must acknowledge that one or two of the collections,

and in particular Aiken's *Twentieth Century American Poetry*, list
to the left somewhat less sharply than the others. But all alike
accentuate work in the prosy tradition of the following:

> I caught a tremendous fish
> and held him beside the boat
> half out of water, with my hook
> fast in a corner of his mouth.
> —Elizabeth Bishop

> The hunchback on the corner, with gums and shoelaces,
> Has his own wisdom and pleasures, and may not be lured
> To divulge them to you, for he has merely endured
> Your appeal for his sympathy and your kind purchases . . .
> —Robert Penn Warren

These examples, neither of which is extreme, illustrate the type
of work that predominates in all five compilations, indicating the
editors' unwillingness or inability to see more than a typographical
distinction between poetry and prose.

But what the anthologists have omitted will tell us as much as
what they have included. Do you find in these five collections so
much as a line by Edwin Markham, author of "The Man with the
Hoe" and other memorable poems? No, not so much as a line! Do
you see any acknowledgement that there was ever a poet named
Arthur Davison Ficke, some of whose sonnets and lyrics are among
the most accomplished of our century? No, you see no such
acknowledgment. Are you treated to even one of the majestic sonnets of George Sterling? Do you make the acquaintance of John G.
Neihardt, who has given us not only some distinguished lyrics but
a series of outstanding rhymed epics of early America? Do you
observe any mention of Sara Teasdale, one of the most accomplished women poets of recent times? Do you find any reference to
Robert Hillyer, Hermann Hagedorn, Lizette Woodworth Reese,
Ridgely Torrence, William Ellery Leonard, and various other representatives of the best in American traditional poetry during this
century? In all these cases, the answer is "No!"

But whatever the gaps in particular books, is not a balance provided by collections chosen on a different basis and including a liberal number of traditionalists? Unfortunately, I have found no indications of any such balance. Although I am acquainted with one personal compilation—Frances Parkinson Keyes' *A Treasury of Favorite Poems,* which is drawn from scrapbooks and includes mostly traditional selections from Shakespeare to Dorothy Parker— I have been unable to discover even one general anthology of the past twenty years which is edited on a broader basis than the volumes considered above or gives even an approach to proportional representation of poets who would have been recognized as such two generations ago. The slighting or rejection of traditionalists, including a long list of gifted writers, appears to be about as nearly unanimous as possible.

And in this, clearly, there is more than a coincidence or a series of coincidences. There is more even than a literary trend. There is a manifest treading of the Party Line. There is a clamping down of a viselike conformity. There is a denial of the freedom to depart from the prescriptions of the reigning clique.

3

The result is so paradoxical as to bring down the laughter of any gods that may still linger on high Parnassus. If you wish suppleness and variety in poetry, if you desire the widest range of tools and of expression, and if you seek the greatest diversity of effects and the utmost freedom, it is not to the innovators that you must turn. In the classical tradition—and in the classical tradition among the writers of our own century—you will find all these things. Consider the varicolored spectrum of possibilities. You may prefer blank verse in the manner of the Canadian poet E. J. Pratt in his long poem, "Brebeuf and His Brethren":

> The winds of God were blowing over France,
> Kindling the hearts and altars, changing vows
> Of rote into an alphabet of flame.

The air was charged with song beyond the range
Of larks, with wings beyond the stretch of eagles.
Skylines unknown to maps broke from the mists
And there was laughter on the seas. . . .

You may choose the style of the airiest of tripping lyrics, as in this
by an American poet, Howard Ramsden:

As on a green hillock
I pluck this wry leaf,
I hear a wee body
To call me a thief.

I see you, Mad Fairy,
As plain as I'd choose.
You sit at yon mullein
To cobble green shoes.

Child of that other land
Under the hill,
Where does Time hurry
The daffodil? . . .

Tell us, the dreamers,
The Lonely, the old—
Where does Time bury
His theft of our gold?

You may prefer epigrammatic rhymed expression, as in these lines
on "Youth and Age" by a contemporary Englishwoman, Eva
Dobell:

When I was young I dreamed Love wore a crown
Of roses, a bright King upon his throne.
Now I am old, I know,—life's pathway trod,—
Love wears a crown,—of thorns,—and Love is God.

You may be captivated by the breathless rush and excitement of a
passage such as this from Victor S. Starbuck's *Saul, King of Israel,*

one of the most colorful and least known of American book-length poems:

> Nahash came, the King of Ammon, with his host against the
>   land,
> And his sword was like the lightning, and his spear was in
>   his hand.
> Those that followed him were many as the stars in Summer
>   sky,
> And their hoofbeats like sea-thunder when the surf is rolling
>   high.

You may be more nearly akin to the spirit of the writers of the great irregular odes, preserving form amid freedom, as does the English poet John Buxton in his thirteen-page "Atropos," whose lines of varying length may be illustrated by the opening passage:

> The world I know must end;
> And after unimaginable time
> Change will have crumbled to the frozen ground
> Mountains and hills, and bound
> In ice the sluggish rivers; and only rime
> Will flower along the meadows. And no tide
> Will move the sea, deep-frozen, where no fish swim.

You may wish to sound the possibilities of unrhymed but rhythmical work not conforming to the pattern of blank verse, as in this from "Hesperian Fall" by Clark Ashton Smith, the California poet who died several years ago:

> The season brings but little gold,
> And only rusty gules and sanguines dull
> To these rude hills with darkling lava cored
> And with thick, somber rocks embossed
> That yield small pasture to the mordant sun;
> And leaves of toneless brown and fawn
> Cluster the glaucous foliage of blue oaks . . .

You may find guidance in flowing rhymeless lines such as those in "Dream," by the late Marion Ethel Hamilton, of San Diego:

What is this dream called life, between sleeping and waking?
This coming from darkness to light, non-being to being?
Life is a gipsy camp—a light upon evil faces—
Death is darkness again, and windy moors in the twilight.

Or you may express yourself with equal flow in a rhymed lyric, as does Ruth Guthrie Harding, of Ridgewood, New Jersey, in her "On a Fly-Leaf of Schopenhauer's *Immortality*":

There is nothing new to be written of tears and man's shud-
        dering breath;
Nothing new to be said of his loving, or sinning, or death;
Nothing new to be thought of his loneliness under the sky—
But something is new in the knowledge that soon it will have
        to be I
Who will give over weeping and breathing, relinquish my
        love and my load,
And lie in the dark and the quiet that waits at the end of
        the road.

The examples might be multiplied almost endlessly, from pre-scribed forms like the sonnet, the rondeau, and the sestina to less formal lyrical measures offering the poet wide discretion and variety. Here, amid rule and order, are diversity and freedom.

But observe by contrast the world of the newer poetry. Let me quote further from the last five anthologies I have listed:

But this, I steadily assure you, is not the world's end,
Nor even the end of a civilization. It is not so late as you
        think: give nature time.
These wars will end, and I shall lead a troupe of shaky old
        men through Europe and America,
Old drunkards, worn-out lechers; fallen dictators, cast-off kings,
        a disgraced president; some cashiered generals . . .   (1)

Dürer would have seen a reason for living
        in a town like this, with eight stranded whales
to look at; with the sweet sea air coming into your house
on a fine day, from water etched
        with waves as formal as the scales
on a fish.   (2)

The lunchroom bus boy who looked like Orson Welles,
Romeo, Brutus, and a man from Mars in his two eyes,
the bellhop who was Joe Louis to the life,
the Greek fruit peddler who in church on Sundays
was a lightning-struck dead image of J. P. Morgan,
the Italian barber who in a mirror was more like
John Barrymore than Barrymore himself,
the Woolworth demonstration cold-cream girl . . .   (3)

Although it is a cold evening,
down by one of the fishhouses
an old man sits netting,
his net, in the gloaming almost invisible,
a dark purple-brown,
and his shuttle worn and polished.
The air smells so strong of codfish
it makes one's nose run and one's eyes water.   (4)

        The people will live on.
The learning and blundering people will live on.
        They will be tricked and sold and again sold
And go back to the nourishing earth for rootholds,
        The people so peculiar in renewal and comeback,
        You can't laugh off their capacity to take it.   (5)

Out there in the dark, what's that horrible chomping?
Oh, nothing, just hogs that forage for mast,
And if you call, "Hoo-pig!" they'll squeal and come romping,
For they'll know from your voice you're the boy who slopped
        them in dear, dead days long past

Any hogs that I slopped are long years dead,
And eaten by somebody and evacuated,
So it's simply absurd, what you said. (6)

These six passages, of course, have their individual differences, as would be the case with any conceivable half-dozen excerpts. But I submit that, although the last of the group uses rhyme and the others do not, they are so similar in method that they might be the products of a single pen. Each proceeds by means of simple statements; each confines itself to matter-of-fact material expressed in the diction of everyday prose; and none rises more than an elbow's length above the earth. Except for some metrical lines in the last quotation, the rhythm is that of prose, and the product would never be mistaken for anything but prose unless printed in a form that labels it "Poetry." Even the last piece, presented without rhyme and the printed looks of poetry, would never be accepted as in the slightest degree poetic.

Then are these six pieces, with their marked similarities, the work of but one writer? The reader, who has doubtless recognized some of them, already knows the answer. The authors are, (1) Robinson Jeffers, in *The Criterion Book of American Verse;* (2) Marianne Moore, in the same; (3) Horace Gregory, in *Twentieth Century American Poetry;* (4) Elizabeth Bishop, in *Modern Verse in English;* (5) Carl Sandburg, in *The New Pocket Anthology of American Verse;* (6) Robert Penn Warren, in *Twentieth Century American Poetry.*

As some of the quotations date back many years, it will be evident that the stereotyped modern style, with its artificial restraints inhibiting the true experimentalism, has been clamped down upon American poetry for a considerable time. Indeed, freedom began to vanish from the moment of the rise of "free verse." For years now only the daring have challenged the ironbound proscriptions against subjectivity, against emotion, against imagination, against flights to the cosmic and against all exaltation, against "clichés" including words such as "beauty" and "truth," against the use of inversions

189

in structure and "poeticisms" and other devices of the older poetry. In some respects, as in the protest against forced and artificial expressions, the revolt does have valid points, although points that affect only superficials—it would not make sense to destroy a house when you need only replace a few rusty nails. The fact is that, while too much heed has been given to the rusty nails, dry rot has been undermining the house of poetry itself.

XIV

OPPORTUNITIES THE MODERNS MISS

I

Being told of treasure buried just beyond the horizon, the ambitious youth went seeking through many lands. He sailed across oceans, climbed mountains, plodded on desert trails, forded rivers, wrestled with jungles, sank in swamps and morasses, and was lost in limitless wastelands. But though he grew old in the quest, he never found what he sought. And he never guessed that, all the while, the treasure lay barely hidden at his own deserted doorstep.

This fable is not without bearing on the plight of present-day poetry. We have seen how our so-called emancipated poets, scorning the ancient subject matter of seas and sunsets and roses and love, have gone threshing far afield in search of new themes. We have noted how, with an obsessive eagerness to be different, they have embraced the trivial, the eccentric, and the repulsive and have tried to make poetry not only out of the prosy details usually found in newspaper items but even out of arithmetical tabulations and statistics. We have observed how, in seeking to prove that there is no area of prose which they cannot enter, the poets have demolished the barriers between poetry and prose, to such an extent that they often leave no distinction between the two except in typographical appearance.

All this is the more extraordinary considering that new material—rich and abundant new material—lies almost unheeded within reach of the modern poet. In no previous era have the world's panoramas expanded so startlingly or provided such fresh opportunities for poetic insight, poetic imagination, and poetic beauty. Let us note some of the possibilities.

2

The first field that comes to mind is the incredible one of twentieth-century science. Here are discoveries that dwarf all the attainments of man's previous fifty or sixty centuries as a civilized being. We need not linger over the well-known facts: the penetrations into infra-universes in the heart of the atom; the revelations of long-past geological ages, when scaly dragons tramped amid steaming fern forests; the observations of galaxies circling beyond galaxies apparently to infinity, each with a complement of billions of worlds, many of which may nourish intelligent life. This material, and much more, has indeed been utilized by writers of science fiction; but the poets, who should take to it like bees to flowers, have in the main appeared unaware of its existence.

True, an occasional poet has nodded acknowledgment of the influence of science. Poe, in an uncharacteristic sonnet, views science with apprehension:

> Hast thou not torn the Naiad from her flood,
> The Elfin from the green grass, and from me
> The summer dream beneath the tamarind tree?

A century after Poe's death another American, Leah Bodine Drake, wrote a sonnet branding science as "The False Messiah," the Judas "Who hammers mankind to the bloody Tree." But this negative interpretation is not the only one possible. Where is the poet who will lift us up among the wheeling suns and portray the mysteries of the universe and of universal life with an imaginative penetration? Where is the poet who will venture into man's remote past and depict our ancestors of the Old Stone Age in all the tenseness and vitality, the peril and terror and marvelous dawn freshness of a life cast among mammoths and cave bears amid the rigors of an ice age? Where is the poet who will give himself to the still greater wonders of our own day, who will celebrate the miracle of space travel, rise with the astronauts, interpret their accomplishments, and illuminate their experience with a vividness beyond any prose report? Here are spurs to the imagination. Here is material that is genuinely new, unhackneyed, and untried. All that we lack is the epic poet.

Nevertheless, there have been some efforts in this direction by traditional poets, including at least one work of imposing dimensions: Alfred Noyes' *The Torch Bearers,* which is devoted mainly to the lives and works of the great scientific originators, the astronomers and mathematicians, biologists and medical researchers. This ambitious poem, written mostly in blank verse, succumbs to the old temptation to descend to long prosy levels; but there are also accomplished passages showing how scientific themes can be adapted to poetry. Upon Galileo's lips the author puts these words:

> Have you not heard, in some great symphony,
> Those golden mathematics making clear
> The victory of the soul?

In lyrical lines Noyes connects the splendors of the starry heavens and the aspirations of mankind:

> I know that I am dust, and daily die;
> Yet, as I trace those rhythmic spheres at night,
> I stand before the Thunderer's throne on high,
> And feast on nectar in the halls of light.

In his song of the Earth, the writer expresses the everlasting hope of watchers of the skies:

> Was it a dream that, in those bright dominions,
> Are other worlds that sing, with lives like mine,
> Lives that with beating hearts and broken pinions
> Aspire and fall, half-mortal, half-divine?

Another poet of this century, California's once widely heralded George Sterling, has likewise ventured with a long poem into the vast spaces of astronomy. His "The Testimony of the Suns," written long before our present information about galaxies and quasars, may be handicapped by its austere, somewhat aloof quality, its remoteness from human passions and struggles. Yet Sterling has shown that his theme can be handled with majesty. Note stanzas such as

> Forever, infinite of range,
>   Unceasing whirls the cosmic storm,
>   In changeless gulfs where Force and Form
> Renew the mystery of Change. . . .

> O Tides that foam on strands untrod
>   From seas in everlasting prime,
>   To light where Life looks forth on Time,
> And Pain, unanswered, questions God!

> What Power, with inclusive sweep
>   And rigor of compelling bars,
>   Shall curb the furies of the stars,
> And still the troubling of that Deep?

Masefield, in his sonnets, makes occasional effective use of astronomical material:

> So in the empty sky the stars appear,
> Are bright in heaven marching through the sky,
> Spinning their planets, each one to his year,
> Tossing their fiery hair until they die . . .

And here, in the following hitherto unpublished piece by Brooks Vaughan (presented by courtesy of the author), we see how the materials of science may be adapted to the needs of poetry:

HALLEY'S COMET

> Once, as a child, I saw its filmy flame
> Point like a ghost along the western sky.

194

Then mutely, with no glimmer of good-bye,
It glided from sight and fame.

Now, for two generations of man's time,
In glooms where even the sun is but a star,
It scales a vault the fleetest atom-car
Never can hope to climb.

And curving back before the century's end,
Changed little in the cold, dark upper blanks,
What shall it witness when our marveling ranks
Watch its long tail extend?

Pray it shall see no continent destroyed,
Cratered by hate, and scorched by crackling gales,
While tranquilly, on everlasting sails,
It floats across the void.

3

Even if much less remote from normal experience than outer
space and not wholly ignored, the theme of air travel has been relatively neglected by our poets. In a sonnet such as Mae Winkler
Goodman's "Night Flight," we get an impression of the poetic
possibilities of the subject:

We leave the ground
to seek a pathway through star-littered skies,
ourselves a star, propelled beyond the bound
of land and sea; here we belong to air . . .

Note how easily this new subject matter is adapted to the older
methods of expression. It would be not more poetic but distinctly
less so and would lose the effect of fluent air movement were it presented in the style of certain antitraditionalists:

We leave the
ground to seek a

pathway through star-
littered skies, ourselves a
star, propelled beyond the
bound of
land and sea.

Possibly even more momentous for our age than air travel is
atomic fission, with its suggestions of a Utopia in which all man's
requirements for energy will be met and he may devote himself to
the expansion of his spirit. Yet that prospect has not been generally
explored by our poets. One reason, of course, is plain: the peril of
the resort to nuclear or thermonuclear devices in warfare. Here, too,
however, is boundless territory for the poetic imagination. But actually this new area has exerted only a limited pull upon our poets,
and again the traditionalists have been foremost in treating this
peculiarly twentieth-century theme. A grim example has been provided by the Nova Scotian poet Watson Kirkconnell in his "After
Atomic Holocaust," which, written in 1958, sees man returned to his
pristine beginnings:

> Our failing flashlights flicker down a shadowy tunnel
> Where skin-clad men once sheltered from the sabre-tooth
> And scratched the mammoth's doom in ochre on the walls.

The poet's reactions to the facts of the nuclear age, on the other
hand, need not be so depressing. A more optimistic position is expressed in a sonnet by Robert Nathan:

> If we must die in bombing and in dust,
> Seeing our cities broken in their pride,
> Then say of us that heaven was our trust,
> Say that we lived in freedom till we died.

But no matter what the point of view, if the poets are to be silent
as to some of the most epoch-making changes since man's discovery
of the use of fire, then poetry will have missed its great opportunity
and forgotten its age-old mission to trumpet forth life's truths with
the voice of the seer and the prophet.

One might suppose that some fabulous power has transported the modern poet to a wonder-realm, where rich themes glisten like jewels in a genie's cave. But the poet enters stooping and eyes downcast, and sees only the dirt on the floor. "This," says he, "is life. This I must portray." And not once does he look up to the vast varicolored brilliant ledges above nor to the gems in their iridescent hues.

This situation, unfortunately, is more than a myth. Consider the bare facts. Even apart from the outright challenge of science and in particular of nuclear power, what do you see if you look out at the modern world? You find that we have passed through the two greatest wars of history and through other portentous conflicts, with epic results for peoples and nations, along with innumerable dramas of courage and endurance, perfidy and treason, devotion and sacrifice. You witness the rise of an assertive and even aggressive nationalism in many lands, the absorption of old political entities, the breach of ancient ties, the formation of new nations. You see the migration and the forced transplantation of peoples and the tragedy of the dispossessed. You observe modern methods and techniques thrust into primitive regions, and continents heaving with the mighty effort at adaptation. You note colonialism in retreat and old colonial territories in chaos, with consequent problems of unparalleled range while some of the nations are startled within by racial tensions inflamed to white heat. In all this, and in the social and industrial conditions of the new age—in the war against poverty, the rise of automation, the battles of capital and labor—do you detect no opportunities for poetry?

The poets themselves provide the answers. They show two things: that there are indeed opportunities, and that those opportunities have in the main been neglected. Consider, for example, the fact that World War I gave the English-speaking world a company of distinguished poets, including Rupert Brooke, Alan Seeger, Wilfred Owen, Charles Hamilton Sorley, Patrick McGill, William Noel

Hodgson, John McCrae, and many others. But during World War II, was there any parallel group? It is well known that there was not. One reason, no doubt, is that the best of the younger poets had been sacrificed in the earlier conflict. Another reason was the mood of weariness, the disillusionment, the apathy, the sheer shock reactions that paralyzed many potential creators. In any event, while much verse did issue from World War II, there was little if any that made a bid to the ages. There was no match for Brooke's eloquent sonnet on the dead:

> These hearts were woven of human joys and cares,
> Washed marvellously with sorrow, swift to mirth.
> The years had given them kindness. Dawn was theirs,
> And sunset, and the colours of the earth.

There was nothing to compare with Siegfried Sassoon's sonnet beginning:

> Soldiers are citizens of death's grey land,
> Drawing no dividend from time's to-morrows.

And there was no equal to the graphic protest of Wilfred Owen's "The Anthem for Doomed Youth":

> What passing-bells for those who died as cattle?
> Only the monstrous anger of the guns.
> Only the stuttering rifles' rapid rattle
> Can patter out their hasty orisons.

These men showed what vivid, feeling work might be evoked by contemporary warfare. Yet these authors found the traditional forms adequate. On the contrary, the English-speaking poets of World War II in large part followed the newer methods, giving us verse in the matter-of-fact mood of this, by Eve Merriam:

> Heroes are supposed to be blond and blue-eyed,
> or tall, dark, and handsome.

And they always get the girl.
Kisses and roses,
the crowd cheering bright as sunlight . . .

Or else we have something in this vein, by one of the more accomplished recent American poets, Stephen Vincent Benét:

Yes, those are voices, playing your old game—
Class against class, ally against ally,
Race against race, smugness against the dream.
A pint of milk a day for every child?
That's a big order—but it isn't silly.

These examples may not illustrate the best poetry of World War II, but they are representative of much. And they indicate how far, within no more than a generation, the poets had sunk in their ability to wrestle with a major theme of the times.

5

The miner deep in the coal pit, hacking away in his need for bread, throws down his pick and swears he must see the sun. . . . The ragged men, unemployed on the streets of a town whose chief industry has moved south, gather in muttering knots to discuss their plight. . . . The youth on probation, finding work in a new community along with high hopes of rehabilitation, is challenged again by the old temptation. . . . The trusted grizzled old employee, bewitched by the call of the racetrack, makes just one more false entry on the books. . . . The member of a minority race, scarred by lifelong discrimination, takes flame against his wrongs. . . . The slum dweller, transferred to polished new housing, sighs for old friends and neighbors. . . . The aging woman, harnessed to an industrial job, dreams of escape. . . . The vigorous old man, in enforced retirement, thrashes against cage walls. . . .

In such themes, supplied by the industrial age, is there not room for poetry? Are there not abundant opportunities to write on sub-

jects largely untouched, provided that the poet can resist the temptation to emphasize ugliness to the neglect of beauty, and provided
also that he is able to strike fire with sparks of poetry? In this effort
even so great a creator as Shelley, criticizing contemporary social
conditions, fell far beneath his characteristic level in his youthful
"Queen Mab," in contrast to this from "Hellas":

> Oh, cease! must hate and death return?
> Cease! must men kill and die?
> Cease! drain not to its dregs the urn
> Of bitter prophecy.
> The world is weary of the past,—
> Oh, might it die or rest at last!

Letitia E. Landon (1802–38), a poet once of wide repute but now
forgotten, was another who cried out against the factories, whose
"dark, funereal" shroud lay over England. But in spite of her work
and that of a few others, including Elizabeth Barrett Browning in
"The Cry of the Children" and Thomas Hood in "The Song of the
Shirt" and "The Bridge of Sighs," the field remained largely virgin
until the approach of our own century. In the work of Gerald Massey, of which we have taken passing note, and in the more accomplished efforts of John Davidson (1857–1909), we see attempts to
put the social problems of the times into poetry, as in the piece
baldly entitled "Thirty Bob a Week" and in the more effective
"Piper, Play!" wherein the author sees brightness amid the gloom:

> Now the furnaces are out,
>   And the aching anvils sleep;
> Down the road the grimy rout
>   Tramples homeward twenty deep.
>   Piper, play! Piper, play!
>   Though we be o'erlaboured men,
>   Ripe for rest, pipe your best!
>   Let us foot it once again!

Not only in his celebrated "The Man with the Hoe" but in various other poems, Edwin Markham attacks the problems of our era. This we may see, for example, in the quatrain "The Third Wonder," with its eloquent line, "The long, long patience of the plundered poor," and likewise in various other poems, such as the one which compares a "labor-blasted" rockbreaker to a pine "on Shasta's top," standing "silent on a cliff,"

> Stript of its glory of green leaves and boughs,
> Its great trunk split by fire,
> Its gray bark blackened by the thunder smoke . . .

The plea of the depressed is likewise sounded in a poem by James Boyd, better known as a novelist, whose "The Black Boys" was written two decades or more before the current wave of civil-rights disturbances:

> Where chimneys cut the sky
> And mill roofs stretch away;
> Where plants' blank walls stand high
> Between the earth and day,
> By woven wire fence,
> At guarded wicket gate,
> Relaxed and yet intense,
> Waiting their known fate,
> Through heat and cold, through rain and shine,
> The black boys stand in line.

Several traditionalists of our age, including John G. Neihardt and Arthur Davison Ficke, have likewise shown that the material of social ferment can be the substance of poetry. In *Tumultuous Shore and Other Poems,* in which he expresses himself as

> out of faith with all
> The vast collective folly of mankind,

Ficke sees

> all the vistas of the heart
> Narrowed to measure of a tradesman's till,

and gives us some of the most feeling poems of the modern city that I have seen—sonnets in which he stares at

> Faces of beauty, faces like damned spirits,
> Faces like leopards, faces like a stone,

and goes on to write,

> He who beholds the million crossing ways
> Of hurried strangers in these thunderous streets,
> Or, half incredulous, pauses to gaze
> Up at the tiers of walls where each repeats,
> Monotonous and unmeaning, all the rest,
> Towering senseless high into multitude—
> He feels the cry of panic in his breast
> And loneliness invades his deepest blood.
> Yet all this is the pattern of a dream.
> The solid fact, even in this haunted place,
> Is but a hand, a voice, a room, a gleam
> Of shaded lights, a well-belovèd face—
> Some personal hour of love or pain or pity:
> These things alone are real. There is no city.

Here the bare facts of the city are transmuted into something profounder than the city—are blended with life's deeper meanings. It is just such a transfusion that one fails to find among poets who have treated advanced themes with "advanced" methods. Compare Ficke's approach with that of Wendell Berry, the holder of a Wallace Stegner Fellowship in Writing at Stanford University and of a Guggenheim Fellowship. The following, from "The Guest," in Allen, Rideout, and Robinson's anthology of *American Poetry,* was written in 1964:

Washed into the doorway
by the wake of the traffic,
he wears humanity
like a third-hand shirt
—blackened with enough
of Manhattan's dirt to sprout
a tree, or poison one.

Again, compare Ficke's writing with that of James Rorty in "Starting from Manhattan":

Riding the neon surf of the city, sucked
By Friday's riptide pouring out
From the hot center, over the bridge,
Into a limbo of BEER and EAT,
Each in his moving cubicle alone
With Bing and Benny . . . Silence
The electronic voices, snap out the lights, and see
What panic could grip these schooled and fated fish!

Or consider a passage such as this, from Pare Lorentz's "The River":

A hundred thousand men to fight the old river.
We sent armies down the river to help the engineers fight a
       battle on a two thousand mile front:
The Army and the Navy,
The Coast Guard and the Marine Corps,
The CCC and the WPA,
The Red Cross and the Health Service.
They fought night and day to hold the old river off the valley.
Food and water needed at Louisville; 500 dead, 5000 ill . . .

There should be no need for further illustrations. The difference between Ficke and writers such as Wendell Berry, James Rorty, and Pare Lorentz is, of course, partly one of technique, but goes far deeper than technique. A more important difference is in the spirit of the work. Ficke brings his whole heart, his whole mind, his whole being to the treatment of modern problems; he does not stand aloof with the cold "objective" approach, but throws his entire self into the discussions, being not only "out of faith with all/The vast collective folly of mankind," but seeing beneath the surface to recognize it all as "the pattern of a dream." Here we have the method and the insight of the poet—the poet who, looking at the world unashamedly through his own eyes, is not content to survey externals of "BEER and EAT" or of "The Coast Guard and the Marine Corps," or to let humanity be worn "like a third-hand shirt."

Not that "BEER and EAT" and "The Coast Guard and the Marine Corps" might not form the subject matter of poetry. But they cannot be made into poetry by merely being enumerated, or by a hard, flat look at the outer realities. It requires something more than this to create poetry; it requires penetration and a warmth of feeling, such as Ficke, Markham, John Davidson, and a few other poets have attained with the materials of modern life. The failure to recognize the need for this all-important element, it seems to me, offers the chief explanation for the relative neglect of the social themes of the age by the self-styled moderns and for the chilling results even in the exceptional cases when such themes are attacked.

XV

MUST WE END IN THE WASTELAND?

For there's a yearning in the dust,
The rich, warm dust of man,
That will be silence if it must,
But music if it can.

Although this thought was phrased by an American of our own day, Richard Kinney, the lines apply to the poets of the ages. Ever since the caveman first uttered a chant to the god of the sun, the moon, or the wind, the fire in the poet's heart has remained much the same. He has sung of the wonder of the world, the pageantry of its cliffs and its streams and its sunsets. He has made melodies of the glory of life and of its pain, of the lover's passion and the mother's bereavement, the jealousy and protection of invisible powers, the sparkling face of a wildflower and the dread countenances of beings believed to ride the clouds or hide beneath the sea. The poet has added a new dimension to life—a dimension beyond the practical, the known, and the seen.

The stage setting, to be sure, has changed with the ages; the stone knife has been replaced by the atom bomb, and the straw hut by the many-towered steel-and-concrete city. But these transformations, while they have given new apparel to the poet's world, have not really altered the poet himself. Beneath whatever garb he has worn, his function has been to make life melodious, to probe beneath its surface to its hidden strangeness and splendor, to unbare veiled beauty, and to disclose truths otherwise unrevealed. Always he has shown that life was greater than it seemed, and that there was more to man than the muscles in his arms or than the spear or the spade which he wielded. The poet has been able, in the words of another contemporary American, Adelaide Love,

> To know what melodies abound
> Even where men hear no sound.

Regardless of modern distractions, this age-old function of the poet remains. It does not matter that he may sit in electrically heated and lighted rooms, listen to voices and see pictures borne to him across the air, or travel in jet planes or self-propelled cars. These are but the externals, and can change the poet only on the surface. In himself he is affected no more than is the man who puts off his workclothes in favor of party attire—at the level of the skin and beneath, nothing whatever has happened to him. In the same way, at the level of the skin and beneath, the poet has not been changed by the fluctuations in society. Nor has the nature of poetry been altered.

These are facts which, it seems to me, have been overlooked in all our talk about "the new movement" and "the new poetry." Essentially, there can be no new poetry, just as there can be no new goodness or truth or beauty; poetry today is what poetry has always been, a basic part of life, and as such it is deeper and more meaningful than all metamorphoses in customs, institutions, and physical appliances; it must either be retained for what it is or else be abandoned under the illusion of reform.

This is not to say that the moods, the tools, and the forms of poetry never change. Shakespeare did not write like Chaucer, nor did Dryden express himself in the manner of Marlowe; each had to adapt his language and his method to the needs of his own personality. The dramatic blank verse of the Elizabethans brought a new element to English poetry, as did the narrative blank verse of Milton, the rhymed couplets of Milton's successors, and the innumerable later individual variations, from the triple-rhymed quatrain which Edward Fitzgerald introduced in *The Rubáiyát* to the *In Memoriam* stanza used by Tennyson. This all represented progress, this all represented experimentation, even if not to the radical extent of abandoning all yesterday's gains and beginning anew as if poetry were a contemporary invention. In the progressives of yesterday we see evolution and not revolution, nor do we find any surrender to the dangerous fallacy that a total break with the past is required by the nature of the present.

This brings us to the basic illogic behind the entire modernistic trend. Poetry, we are told, should express itself in the forms and in the idiom of our era; its garb should be adapted to our era; it should reflect the agitation, the nervousness, the conflict, the confusion of today. This, although it has been accepted as almost axiomatic, is as perfect a non sequitur as you could find. It is like saying that, if a man goes to work feeling in a gala mood, he should dress like a clown; or if he is depressed, he should clothe himself like a mourner at a funeral. The delusion revolves about the idea that the apparel is all-important, that the forms are what count most, that the paraphernalia of poetic expression take precedence over the things expressed, and that phenomena such as nervousness, conflict, and confusion can best be made known by changes in the garb rather than in the substance. That this idea is not only mistaken but absurd can be shown by a simple example. Consider these familiar lines from *Hamlet:*

> I am thy father's spirit,
> Doom'd for a certain term to walk the night,
> And for the day confin'd to fast in fires,
> Till the foul crimes done in my days of nature
> Are burnt and purg'd away. But that I am forbid
> To tell the secrets of my prison house,
> I could a tale unfold whose lightest word

Would harrow up thy soul, freeze thy young blood,
Make thy two eyes, like stars, start from their spheres,
Thy knotted and combin'd locks to part,
And each particular hair to stand on end,
Like quills upon the fretful porpentine . . .

Here, if anywhere, we have disturbance and confusion, shot
through with terror. But is the form of expression confused or disturbed? Not at all! We have the smooth and rhythmic sweep of the
blank verse, all the more effective because it does not distract one's
attention by a distorted or fractured style. Observe how, far from
adding to the troubled effect, the style would call attention to itself
at the expense of the meaning and detract from the high seriousness
of the whole had the author written, in the modern manner:

I am your father's *fantôme* * * *
Mon Dieu! Mon Dieu! Un revenant! ! !
A night-walker, a night-walker, a night-
walker . . . doomed
by day . . . shades of great Caesar!
confined to fast in fires—curses on the crimes
done before you cashed in my life policy!—
If it wasn't for the damned censorship
what I could tell you, boy,
would sure make you hop . . .

Need one go on? Here, certainly, we have a nervous, a disturbed
style. But do the nervousness, the disturbance of the form add to the
poetic effect?

2

When the modern farmer sows and reaps, he does not discard the
tractor or the harvesting machine and experiment with the hand-
driven wooden plow or the primitive pruning hook. When the
engineer plans a bridge, he does not scorn the teachings of physics
and mathematics and the experience of previous bridge-builders as

to stress and strain; nor does he start all over again as if no bridge had ever been built before. And when the scientist explores the depths of the galaxies or the heart of the atom, he does not ignore what earlier astronomers and physicists have taught him, but attempts to advance from where they left off.

Quite different, however, has been the case with our modern poets. For them poetry, in effect, is an art without ancestry, an art that originated with themselves and their immediate preceptors. The slowly acquired experience of three thousand years, the fruit of previous experimentation from *The Iliad* and before, to *The Everlasting Mercy* of Masefield, has been quietly ignored. Chaucer and Spenser, Shakespeare and Milton, Gray and Coleridge and Wordsworth and Keats and Shelley and all the poets of the great old line might never have written for all that one can judge from the formless, mostly rhymeless, rhythmless, frequently dissociated and obscure, predominantly prosy work such as we have examined. Poetry might never have been the medium for soaring thought, scintillating fancy, exalted imagination, song and splendor and beauty and moving emotion. Indeed, the apostles of the new movement have begun as might a tribe of aborigines, who, having just invented writing, have conceived the idea of poetry for the first time and are investigating its possibilities without benefit of any guidelines.

Paradoxically, however, this return to the primitive is not a new phenomenon. It began in the English-speaking world as far back as the Imagists of the second decade of this century, and even as long ago as Stephen Crane (1871–1900). Thus the movement, originally termed "experimental," although "nihilistic" would have been a truer designation, has long ago passed beyond experimentation to petrifaction—a petrifaction that is the negation of genuine experimentalism.

This is true despite the various schools of rebels and the crosscurrents within their camps. Although one cannot bracket the relatively mild Amy Lowell with the more radical Ezra Pound and T. S. Eliot, and although the earlier insurgents did not mutilate the language as did some of their successors, nevertheless one principle may be seen behind them all: a turning from the past, a scorn for past models, an attempt to transform poetry into something new, something different than ever before, something owing no debt to preceding centuries.

This, I submit, was an impossibility, just as it would be impossible for law or medicine or horticulture to cast aside everything learned before the twentieth century. But this, while it has parallels in the other arts, has gone further in poetry than in the other arts—further in removing poetry as it was recognized yesterday from the view of audiences today. In painting, whatever the extremes of certain artists, the vogue of Picasso, Matisse, and others of the new school has not caused the work of El Greco, Raphael, and Rembrandt to be crated away to the basements of museums as a means for providing wall space for their successors. In music, whatever the innovations of Bartok or Shostakovich, concert audiences and the owners of hi-fi sets still listen to Bach, Handel, and Mozart (in fact, according to a recent note by Herbert Kupferberg in *The Atlantic,* more recordings by Mozart are in existence than by any other composer). But in poetry the emphasis, as we have seen in the case of recent anthologies, is so decisively upon the new that a reader might be unaware that the art had not begun with *The Waste Land.* In poetry there is more than an attempt to introduce new methods; there is an intolerant, a dictatorial endeavor to squeeze out everything except the new methods and their representatives.

None of this, as I have pointed out, should be taken to mean that we must confine our vision to the horizons of our ancestors. No generation, except in a stagnant world, need be or can be a carbon copy of preceding generations. But this does not imply that any generation must blast away the previous artistic methods—merely that it must put forth new shoots upon the old bough. While I personally do not hold that any single technical device apart from a regular rhythm is indispensable for the poet, I can see no reason to throw overboard resources which for centuries have proved their value— not unless, as is definitely not the case, they can be shown to have lost all usefulness. Nor do I think it possible to achieve poetry by abandoning at one reckless toss *all* the methods by which all the classical poets attained their ends. This represents no constructiveness or progress. This represents anarchy—an anarchy in which, as when bad currency drives out good according to the economic principle known as Gresham's Law, the false poetry expels the true, until it has taken over the field and only the weeds and tares remain.

But what of freedom? Should we deny the poet's right to express himself as he desires? Unfortunately, there has been a vast amount of confusion in this regard and a failure to recognize that freedom has its own dictates, which can be flouted only at the risk of anarchy.

All great creators, of course, have responded to the laws of their own beings. Chaucer responded to those laws in weaving his marvelous tales, Spenser in entering into the enchanted allegorical domains of his long fairy poem, Shakespeare in the vast sweep of his plays and in the emotional drive of the great moments that bade the winds to "crack" their cheeks or made the characters somber with predictions of "tomorrow and tomorrow and tomorrow." Pope responded to the laws of his own being in his neat and ironic epigrams, Wordsworth in steeping himself in the glories of nature and of a time when "meadow, grove and stream" to him did seem "Apparelled in celestial light," Shelley in crying out to the west wind with a passion felt by few, "O! lift me as a wave, a leaf, a cloud! . . . Make me thy lyre, even as the forest is."

And so on and on throughout a long list, which includes every notable poet who ever set pen to verse before our own day. All were free; all made use of their freedom to express the distinctive traits of their own personalities. But while unrestricted in pouring forth the unique and peculiar values within themselves, they nevertheless felt invisible barriers, which cried out, "You must not trespass!" And those barriers were prescribed not only by the technique of their art but by the canons of reasonableness and self-discipline considered normal in human affairs. Milton, though a great innovator in the use he made of English poetry, would not have felt that the right of innovation entitled him to address the Deity in the familiar, patronizing, or insulting manner of certain moderns. The poets of the Restoration, whatever their religious convictions or lack of convictions, would not have expressed their freedom by sprinkling their verse with profanity or with splashes of gutter filth, in the manner of some of the present avant-garde. Swinburne, amid the resigned pessimism of his mellifluous "The Garden of Proserpine," even while gloomily declaring that "And well though love reposes,/In the end it is not well," and foreseeing "Only the sleep eternal/In an eternal night," is far from translating the chaos which he feels into chaotic language. And Keats, amid the bleakness of "a drear-nighted December" or the horrid witchcraft of "La Belle Dame Sans Merci," never for one syllable departs from the precepts of melodious expression. Through freedom restrained by law, these creators have given us poetry no matter what their personal convictions and no matter what the world's disorder. Through freedom unrestrained by law, they could only have led us into the wilderness.

3

Sometimes, when one reads "modern" selections such as I have quoted throughout these pages—selections which, far from representing their authors' worst, often leave out of account their ugliest and most offensive aberrations—one cannot repress the suspicion that the writers have not much love nor even much respect for poetry. Chiefly one receives this impression from the way in which they treat poetry as a fit subject for acrobatic exhibitions, jarring rhythms, distortions of words and meanings, and various other eccentricities. But in some instances the poets, by their direct statements, make one question the depth of their devotion to the art they profess to honor. This is the case when Richard Ashman, writing in the poetry magazine *Compass Review,* announces that "I am a poet, but I never write." And it is no less true when Tony Macchia, co-editor of *Asterick,* contributes the following to his magazine:

Just because
I must write

a little bit
of poetry
Is it good, is it bad?
That doesn't matter . . .

It would be easy to put too much emphasis on these remarks by little-known writers in obscure journals, even though they do illustrate a trend. Nor need one consider that Wallace Stevens is being more than merely casual when he writes, "Poetry is the supreme fiction, madame." One cannot, however, so lightly wave aside Archibald MacLeish's often-quoted statements in his "Ars Poetica"—statements that draw their significance not only from what they say as to their author but from the wide approval accorded them:

A poem should be palpable and mute
As a globed fruit. . . .

A poem should be wordless
As the flight of birds. . . .

A poem should be equal to:
Not true. . . .

A poem should not mean
But be.

These generalities, of course, are self-contradictory. One thing that a poem should not be, in fact cannot be—one thing which "Ars Poetica" itself is not—is mute and wordless. One thing that a poem should be is true. And if "Ars Poetica" is not true, what worth has it? As for not meaning—if a poem does not mean, how can it be? And why, in that event, should it be? Moreover, does not MacLeish's offering attempt to mean in the very act of saying it should not mean?

Thus, however you analyze it, this poem shows a limiting, an unrealistic, yes, a nonsensical attitude toward poetry. From such an attitude, none of the memorable poems of other days have arisen, for they all—down to the lightest of light lyrics—have sought to mean as well as to be.

As a further example, observe these remarks by the British poet Christopher Hassell in his poem "The Burden Within":

> The poetry comes less from the words themselves than from
> our own thoughts toying with the practical impli-
> cations involved in
> *The burden, dispersedly, within, BOW-WOW.*

The italics are the author's own. The last line, for even greater emphasis, is used five times as a refrain.

But if this shows a disdainful attitude toward poetry, it is outdone by the confession of Marianne Moore:

> I, too, dislike it: there are things that are important beyond
> all this fiddle.
> Reading it, however, with a perfect contempt for it, one
> discovers in
> it after all, a place for the genuine.

In the same class are the lines of William Carlos Williams in "Paterson":

> Give up
> the poem. Give up the shilly-
> shally of art.

Such passages, it seems to me, are revealing, since the state of any art depends to a large extent upon the state of mind of its creators. If the creators hold that poetry is "fiddle" and art is "shilly-shally," if, in fact, they are not convinced that what they are doing is supremely important, then their output is unlikely to have much importance for others. If Michelangelo had not felt the superlative value of the frescoes in the Sistine Chapel or of the statues in the

Medici Chapel or of his sculptured David or Moses, then surely the world would never have known the preeminent art that is associated with his name. If Beethoven had for a moment thought that the making of harmonious sounds was a fit subject for contempt, then we would never have had the Fourth Piano Concerto or the Ninth Symphony. And so on throughout all art and all literature. Great creation occurs only when the creators devotedly believe in the worth of what they are doing. And the present age can be no exception. When the attitude of the times, as reflected in its artists, is jejune, disillusioned, cynical, or scornful, then masterpieces are automatically ruled out. In this fact, I believe, one will find a prime reason why the modernist poets have descended not only beneath greatness but beneath poetry, and sometimes beneath prose and occasionally beneath language, and why we can thumb through page after page of the reputed modern masters, such as T. S. Eliot, Marianne Moore, William Carlos Williams, and Ezra Pound, without discovering a single passage, even if one can find an isolated line, that takes fire from a recognizable poetic impulse.

4

Despite the perversions that have increasingly obscured much that is best and worthiest of attention, one of the dominant facts about poetry in this century, as I have repeatedly indicated, is the abundance and the quality of much of the production both in America and in Great Britain. In the latter country, there are, first of all, the recognized giants: Yeats, Masefield, de la Mare, A. E. Housman, Robert Bridges, and Thomas Hardy—not all of whom, however, are wholly of this century. And to these one may possibly add one or two others, including the Irish mystic "A.E." and Alfred Noyes, whose work, now under something of a shadow, may yet surge back to attention. In addition, there are many accomplished poets, some of them widely known and others more or less unfamiliar: Gerald Bullett, Vera Brittain, Lord Dunsany, John Drinkwater, James Elroy Flecker, Francis Ledwidge, Sylvia Lynd, Laurence Housman, Gerald Gould, A. C. Benson, V. Sackville-West, W. H. Davies,

Lascalles Abercrombie, Edmund Blunden, Laurence Binyon, Wilfrid Wilson Gibson, Frederick Manning, Lucy Lyttleton, Sheila Kaye-Smith, Geoffrey Johnson, Gilbert Thomas, Wilfrid Thorley, J. C. Squire, S. R. Lysaght, Phoebe Hesketh, Thomas Ansell, R. L. Cook, John Buxton, Lady Wentworth, P. D. Cummins, E. V. Rieu, R. W. Moore, Vivian Locke Ellis, Gilbert Keith Chesterton, Charles Williams, and many others, including the poets of the First World War. But a mere catalogue of names means little: let me give one or two examples of the work of some of the less widely acclaimed British poets of this century. Here, for example, is a quatrain by the author of many able lyrics, Lady Margaret Sackville:

> The fire burned low: fast fell the curtained gloom:
> I thought: How well the Silence understands,
> Who, tenderly maternal, fills the room
> With unobtrusive touch of healing hands.

And here is another four-line offering by the same poet:

> Not the cold grip of suffocating Time
> Which takes the ardent spirit unawares,
> Shall shake thy faith—the faith that bids thee climb
> This ladder of steep light whose steps are prayers . . .

In these short poems we have the compression, the imagination, the feeling, the controlled rhythm, the suggestiveness, the aptness of phrasing, the vision of poetry. But these are the sort of poems which, though far from few in number, have been generally overlooked in favor of work that sounds like prose altered (though not much altered) or like a form of subprose.

Let me present a further example. Not many readers today, I suspect, know the name of the Welsh poet A. G. Prys-Jones. Yet he is the author of some lyrics of rare singing quality, as well as of some notable descriptions of his native countryside, of which the following is from a short piece entitled "The Ploughman" and subtitled "In Welsh Uplands":

Here did his fathers live and pass
    To slumber after ceaseless toil,
Sealing beneath the springing grass
    Their silent epic of the soil.

For there they tilled and hardly won
    From out the slow and stubborn weald
In murk and mist and kindlier sun
    These acres and their scanty yield.

And here he stands, as oft they stood,
    Untutored in the Saxon speech,
Driving his furrows from the wood
    Down to the long, low river-reach.

His words are few and few his needs,
    He seeks no quarrel with his kind,
And silence deeper silence breeds
    Within the mazes of his mind.

Now, for its telling summation in a few singing lines of the feelings and the philosophy of a lifetime, read "On the Sea-Front," by the English poet and critic Gilbert Thomas:

The long day comes full circle.
    Its early light returns.
What all have heard as theory
    Each in his own time learns.

For me the hours are rounding.
    Never might there have been
Noon's dazzle that was darkness:
    So clear again the scene.

Splendour has wheeled to splendour.
    Though broken appeared the ring,
Sunset completes the sunrise
    That made my childhood sing.

The cycle is accomplished.
Present fulfils the past
As, through the glare of custom,
Wonder leaps back at last.

The long day comes full circle.
I look. I gasp. Once more
I stare, like any infant,
At sky and sea and shore.

Limitations of space, unfortunately, will not permit further quotations from the abundant British sources. Let me therefore turn to America, where there has likewise been a burgeoning of poetry, even though one would find no intimations of the fact in most contemporary publications. I have already quoted from some recent American poets, and have named many meritorious and once-noted writers who have been omitted from recent anthologies. But many more, some of whom once attained a measure of recognition while others are almost totally unknown, are deserving of attention. To present the complete list would be impossible, although I could fill a page with names. But let me make one or two quotations from poets whom we tend to overlook nowadays as outside the prescribed groove. Consider "Morning Is All I Want," by Louise Townsend Nicholl:

I would die happiest in ardent light
With every petal of the life unfurled,
The sunlight drawing to its final height
My long intense alliance with the world.

Morning is all I want, the rapture lying
Abundant and immeasurably bright—
Reality so pure that even dying
Must wear the face of morning and of light.

While Miss Nicholl is fortunate compared with some of her brothers and sisters, and has achieved various recognitions and been published by some of our most reputable houses, the extent of her audience may be gauged from the fact that her *Collected Poems* (1953) was issued in a limited edition of 746 copies.

Let us glance at another example. In "Footsteps," by Otto Freund, who some years ago contributed well-wrought and feeling poems to various national magazines but has since disappeared from the world of poetry, we find a theme that is both modern and timeless:

> All day I hear them tapping in the street,
>   The footsteps passing by;
> Like castanets their quick crescendos beat,
>   And quickly die.
>
> On futile errands pressing to and fro
>   Their echoes never cease;
> In madness some, in sorrow others go,
>   But none in peace.
>
> Their owners blind, the misty goals they see
>   Before them gleam and fade,
> Like crumbling domes of wind-built fantasy,
>   By winds decayed.
>
> All day they go, the feet that never rest
>   From fruitless, drab affairs,
> Till night brings forth the stars, in silent quest
>   As vain as theirs.

Likewise timeless in its depth and implications, as well as distinctive in theme and warmly human in its sympathies, is "Slave Cemetery," by Minnie Hite Moody, a Georgia poet and novelist widely published in periodicals:

> Let the mimosa droop where they are sleeping,
> Lijah and Enoch, Deborah and Sue,
> Vashti and Sam. It is in keeping
> That they should rest, with no more work to do.

At long, long last, here are the lazy days;
The very seasons falter, passing by,
And clouds drift in a thousand different ways
Across the gentle arch of Georgia sky.
A century has passed since they were scolded
Or praised or blamed or hurried or cajoled;
Theirs is eternal peace, with tired hands folded,
And ours the heartache for the bought and sold,
However deep in rest they seem to be
Under the drooping green mimosa tree.

Here is the sort of poetry which, unless we let it be obliterated by
shallow, formless, and prosy vaporings (as is already happening)
may form the basis of an enduring American literature.

5

Although one may be encouraged by the amount of good and even
distinguished work accomplished during this century by American
and British poets, the disquieting fact is that this work is largely con-
centrated in the earlier decades and becomes much sparser as one
moves toward midcentury and past. Disquieting also is the fact that,
while posing pygmies are paraded as "great," most current periodicals
and anthologies and individual books of verse, and likewise the
awards of prize committees, give you no idea at all of the existence
of much of the best modern poetry, if indeed they introduce you to
any poetry whatever. But perhaps still more disquieting is the evidence that, thanks to the straitjacket clamped down by the legisla-
tors of novelty and the widespread teaching of the narrow contemporary creed in schools and colleges, we are drifting on a rapid current away from respect for the great models of the past and are
losing all desire to emulate or surpass those models.

In poetry, of course, as in most things, there are fads and fashions.
In poetry, as in other fields, men rarely question the correctness of
the conformer (who in this case, paradoxically, is the supposed rebel,
while the traditionalist is the true insurgent). In poetry, even as in

society, business, and politics, the majority hasten to join the crowd, lest their actions should in the slightest degree become distinguishable from those of others. Thus powerful forces making toward uniformity—a sheepish uniformity in the name of freedom—constitute a chief reason why jolting, flat, ice-cold, unimaginative, visionless, and often opaque, pretentious, distorted work has taken so strong a hold. It is these forces that, as I mentioned in the beginning, have insured that, while poetry as a living voice has almost ceased to be heard in favor of pseudopoetry, no protests are being raised. Hence these forces, if unchecked, will lead us into the wasteland—a wasteland from which, as from the desert into which poetry sank in ancient Rome after the golden age of Virgil, Ovid, and Horace, there may be little prospect of recovery for centuries.

This descent, however, need not occur. And it will not occur if we awaken to the realities; if we strike out against the powers choking creativity and censoring rhymed and metrical expression out of existence. The first necessity is true freedom in poetry, in place of the pseudofreedom preached by the new movement. Poetry should be confined to no one group, school, or outlook; its mansions should be open enough and broad enough for all who approach them sincerely. I see no reason why writers should not be permitted any philosophy or any artistic approach which they accept honestly and not as a trick or hoax or exhibitionistic pose or opportunistic display and which they do not try to enforce upon others. I see no reason why they should not experiment—so long as experiments are labeled by their own name, and are not assumed to be synonymous with attainment, and seek no dictatorial disbarment of opposing experiments or of divergent points of view. I see no reason, furthermore, why acceptance of the new should mean rejection of the old, nor why vigorous young growth cannot exist side by side with luxuriant earlier developments, as when, in a forest, seedlings and saplings shoot up about the stately parental columns. Above all, my plea is for tolerance and justice—the tolerance and justice now resolutely and self-righteously denied to those who cannot see eye to eye with the innovators, the tolerance and justice without which we are in peril of losing forever a great mass of excellent and even superb work produced by the poets of our century.

But with such tolerance and justice we may go far toward repairing the grave mistakes of the recent past. With a recognition that poetry may be modern and yet may use techniques familiar to Wordsworth and Shelley, with an understanding that creative fulfillment is not possible beneath the pressure of arbitrary laws or in the face of dogmas and injunctions whether or not they are called free or modern, we may be on the way to making poetry once more a vestibule to the courts of the gods rather than an exhibition ground for circus performers.

That we have reached a crucial stage I have not the slightest doubt, nor that the time for realization is now—now, before the tides of intolerance have become irreversible and the glories and blessings of poetry's long past will be sunken like the towers of fabled Atlantis, drowned by the floods of the cold prose of an uncreative age.

Perhaps the following lines—lines not original in their thought or expression although sincere in their conviction—will give a better idea than my prose utterances why, in my view, the encouragement of the singer and the preservation of his song are of outstanding importance:

One seeker, rumbling with an earthquake tread,
Shouted in bleeding towns his steeled commands;
And conquered, while he struck whole empires dead,
A thousand lands.

And one, unnoted, chose instead the boon
Of lyric splendor; sang of vision and tears;
And conquered, by the sorcery of his tune,
A thousand years.

BIBLIOGRAPHY

(Modern works cited, and sources of modern poems)

Compilations

American Poetry, edited by Gay Wilson Allen, Walter B. Rideout, and James K. Robinson, Harper & Row, New York, 1966.

An Anthology of Famous English and American Poets, edited, with Introduction, by William Rose Benét and Conrad Aiken, The Modern Library, New York, 1945.

Best Poems of 1956, Borestone Mountain Poetry Awards, 1957, Stanford University Press, Stanford University, Calif., 1957.

Best Poems of 1960, Borestone Mountain Poetry Awards, 1961, Pacific Books, Palo Alto, Calif., 1962.

The Book of American Negro Poetry, edited by James Weldon Johnson, Harcourt, Brace & Co., New York, 1922.

The Bronze Treasury, edited by Harry Kemp, The Macaulay Company, New York, 1927.

The Conscious Voice, An Anthology of American Poetry from the Seventeenth Century to the Present, edited by Albert D. Van Nostrand and Charles H. Watts, Jr., The Liberal Arts Press, New York, 1959.

A Controversy of Poets, edited by Paris Leary and Robert Kelly, Anchor Books, Doubleday & Co., Garden City, N.Y., 1965.

The Criterion Book of Modern American Verse, edited, with Introduction, by W. H. Auden, Criterion Books, New York, 1956.

The Golden Treasury of Scottish Poetry, selected and edited by Hugh MacDiarmid, The Macmillan Company, New York, 1941.

The Modern Poets, An American-British Anthology, edited by John Malcolm Brinnin and Bill Read, McGraw-Hill Book Company, New York, 1963.

Modern Verse in English, 1900–1950, edited by David Cecil and Allen Tate, The Macmillan Company, New York, 1958.

The Moment of Poetry, edited by Don Cameron Allen, Johns Hopkins University Press, Baltimore, 1962.

Mother, edited by Katie May Gill, Cavalier Press, Richmond, Va., 1957.

The New American Poetry: 1945–1960, edited by Donald M. Allen, Grove Press, New York, 1960.

A New Anthology of Modern Poetry, edited, with Introduction, by Selden Rodman, The Modern Library, New York, 1946.

The New Pocket Anthology of American Verse, from Colonial Days to the Present, edited by Oscar Williams, The Pocket Library, New York, 1955.

New Poems 1961, A P.E.N. Anthology of Contemporary Poetry, edited by William Plomer, Anthony Twaite, and Hilary Cooke, Hutchinson and Company, London, 1961.

New Poems 1963, A British P.E.N. Anthology, edited by Lawrence Durrell, Harcourt, Brace & World, Inc., New York, 1964.

The New Poetry, edited by Harriet Monroe and Alice Corbin Henderson, The Macmillan Company, New York, 1923.

New World Writing 19, L. B. Lippincott Company, Philadelphia and New York, 1961.

100 American Poems, edited by Selden Rodman, The New American Library, New York, 1948.

The Oxford Book of American Verse, chosen and edited by Bliss Carman, Oxford University Press, New York, 1927.

The Oxford Book of Canadian Verse in English and French, chosen and with Introduction by A. J. M. Smith, Toronto, 1960.

The Pocket Book of Modern Verse, edited by Oscar Williams, Pocket Books, Inc., New York, 1954.

The Pocket Companion, edited, with Introduction, by Philip Van Doren Stern, Pocket Books, New York, 1942.

Poems of Doubt and Belief, An Anthology of Modern Religious Poetry, edited by Tom F. Driver and Robert Pack, The Macmillan Company, New York, 1964.

Poetry Awards, 1952, University of Pennsylvania Press, Philadelphia, 1952.

Poet's Choice, edited by Paul Engle and Joseph Lagland, The Dial Press, New York, 1962.

Poets of Today, Vol. VIII, Albert Herzing, John M. Ridland, David R. Slavitt, Charles Scribner's Sons, New York, 1961.

Poets of Today, edited by Walter Lowenfels, International Publishers, New York, 1964.

A Treasury of Favorite Poems, edited by Frances Parkinson Keyes, Hawthorn Books, New York, 1963.

Twentieth Century American Poetry, edited by Conrad Aiken, Modern Library, New York, 1963.

War Poems of the United Nations, edited by Joy Davidman, Dial Press, New York, 1943.

Critical Works

W. H. Auden, in Introduction to Poems of Alfred Lord Tennyson, Doubleday, Doran & Co., Inc., Garden City, N.Y., 1944.

C. M. Bowra, The Creative Experiment, The Macmillan Company, New York, 1949.

Glauco Cambon, The Inclusive Flame, Studies in American Poetry, Indiana University Press, Bloomington, 1963.

Howard Willard Cook, Our Poets of Today, Moffat, Yard & Company, New York, 1923.

David Daiches, Literary Essays, Philosophical Library, New York, 1957.

Babette Deutsch, Poetry in Our Time, Henry Holt & Company, New York, 1952.

David Holbrook, Dylan Thomas and Poetic Dissociation, Preface by Harry T. Moore, Southern Illinois University Press, Carbondale, 1964.

John Holmes, in The Moment of Poetry, edited by Don Cameron Allen, The Johns Hopkins Press, Baltimore, 1962.

J. Isaacs, The Background of Modern Poetry, E. P. Dutton & Company, New York, 1952.

F. R. Leavis, New Bearings in English Poetry, University of Michigan Press, Ann Arbor, 1960.

John Livingston Lowes, Convention and Revolt in Poetry, Houghton Mifflin Company, Boston, 1919.

Theodore Maynard, Preface to Poetry, The Century Company, New York, 1933.

Gilbert Murray, The Classical Tradition in Poetry, Harvard University Press, Cambridge, 1927.

Charles Norman, *The Magic-Maker E. E. Cummings,* The Macmillan Company, New York, 1958.
Herbert Read, *The Nature of Literature,* The Grove Press, New York, 1958.
Russell Hope Robbins, *The T. S. Eliot Myth,* Henry Schuman, New York, 1951.
M. L. Rosenthal, *The Modern Poets, A Critical Introduction,* Oxford University Press, New York, 1960.
Stephen Spender, *The Struggle of the Modern,* University of California Press, Berkeley and Los Angeles, 1963.
Allen Tate, *On the Limits of Poetry,* The Swallow Press and William Morrow & Company, New York, 1948.
John Hall Wheelock, *What Is Poetry?,* Charles Scribner's Sons, New York, 1963.

Individual Volumes and Poems

A.E., *Collected Poems,* Macmillan & Co., Ltd., London, 1931.
Conrad Aiken, *A Letter from Li Po and Other Poems,* Oxford University Press, New York, 1955.
———, *The Morning Song of Lord Zero,* Oxford University Press, New York, 1963.
Daisy Aldan, *The Destruction of Cathedrals and Other Poems,* Two Cities Press, Paris and New York, 1963.
W. H. Auden, *Collected Poetry,* Random House, New York, 1945.
———, *About the House,* Random House, New York, 1965.
Arno L. Bader and Carlton F. Wells, *Essays of Three Decades,* Harper & Bros., New York, 1939.
Stephen Vincent Benét, "Dear Adolf," in Joy Davidman's *War Poems of the United Nations.*
John Berryman, *77 Dream Songs,* Farrar, Straus and Giroux, New York, 1964.
Frederick Bock, *The Fountain of Regardlessness,* The Macmillan Company, New York, 1961.
James Boyd, *Eighteen Poems,* Charles Scribner's Sons, New York, 1944.
Kay Boyle, *Collected Poems,* Alfred A. Knopf, New York, 1962.
Rupert Brooke, *Collected Poems,* John Lane Company, London and New York, 1915.
Gwendolyn Brooks, *The Bean Eaters,* Harper & Bros., New York, 1960

——, *A Street in Bronzeville,* Harper & Bros., New York, 1945.

John Buxton, *Atropos and Other Poems,* Macmillan & Co., Ltd., London, 1946.

Witter Bynner (Emmanuel Morgan, pseudonym) and Arthur Davison Ficke (Anne Knish, pseudonym), *Spectra, A Book of Poetic Experiments,* Mitchell Kennerley, New York, 1916.

Warren Carrier, *Toward Montebello,* Harper & Row, New York, 1966.

Hayden Carruth, *Nothing for Tigers, Poems 1959–1964,* The Macmillan Company, New York, 1965.

John Ciardi, *In the Stoneworks,* Rutgers University Press, New Brunswick, N.J., 1961.

——, *39 Poems,* Rutgers University Press, New Brunswick, N.J., 1959.

Pauline Avery Crawford, *Sonnets From A Hospital,* Bruce Humphries, Inc., Boston, 1936.

E. E. Cummings, *Collected Poems,* Harcourt, Brace & Co., New York, 1938.

——, *95 Poems,* Harcourt, Brace & Co., New York, 1958.

——, *Xaipe: seventy-one poems,* Oxford University Press, New York, 1950.

John Davidson, *Poems,* Introduction by R. M. Wenley, Boni & Liveright, 1924.

James Dickey, *Buckdancer's Choice,* Wesleyan University Press, 1966.

Eva Dobell, in *Wings, A Quarterly of Verse,* Vol. XIII, No. 4, Winter, 1958.

Leah Bodine Drake, in *Wings, A Quarterly of Verse,* Vol. IX, No. 1, Spring, 1949.

Alan Dugan, *Poems,* Foreword by Dudley Fitts, Yale University Press, New Haven, 1961.

Robert Duncan, *The Opening of the Field,* The Grove Press, New York, 1960.

Lawrence Durrell, *Selected Poems,* The Grove Press, New York, 1956.

Richard Eberhart, *Selected Poems, 1930–1965,* New Directions, New York, 1965.

T. S. Eliot, *Collected Poems, 1909–1962,* Harcourt, Brace and World, New York, 1963.

Paul Engle, *American Child,* Random House, New York, 1945.

Kenneth Fearing, *Afternoon of a Pawnbroker*, Harcourt, Brace & Company, New York, 1943.

Thomas Hornsby Ferrill, *New and Selected Poems*, Harper & Bros., New York, 1952.

Arthur Davison Ficke, *Tumultuous Shore and Other Poems*, Alfred A. Knopf, Inc., New York, 1942.

Wilfrid Wilson Gibson, *Neighbors*, The Macmillan Company, New York, 1920.

William Gibson, *Winter Crook*, Oxford University Press, New York, 1948.

Allen Ginsberg, *Howl for Carl Solomon*, City Lights Books, San Francisco, 1956.

Mae Winkler Goodman, *Verge of Eden*, New and Selected Poems, The Devin-Adair Company, New York, 1962.

Robert Graves, *Collected Poems*, Doubleday & Co., Garden City, N.Y., 1961.

Horace Gregory, *Medusa in Gramercy Park*, The Macmillan Company, New York, 1961.

Marion Ethel Hamilton, *Bird at Night*, The Fine Editions Press, New York, 1949.

Ruth Guthrie Harding, in *Wings, A Quarterly of Verse*, Vol. VI, No. 5, Spring, 1944.

Christopher Hassell, *The Red Leaf*, Oxford University Press, London, 1957.

Lafcadio Hearn, *Selected Writings*, edited by Henry Goodman, The Citadel Press, New York, 1949.

Terence Heywood, *How Smoke Gets into the Air*, The Fortune Press, London, n.d.

Doris Holmes, in *Saturday Review*, January 7, 1967.

Gerard Manley Hopkins, *Poems*, 3rd ed., edited by W. A. Gardner, Oxford University Press, New York and London, 1948.

W. H. Hudson, *A Crystal Age*, E. P. Dutton & Co., New York, 1917.

Ted Hughes, *The Hawk in the Rain*, Harper & Bros., New York, 1957.

John Irvine, *Selected Poems*, The Arden Press, London, 1948.

Randall Jarrell, *The Lost World*, The Macmillan Company, New York, 1965.

Robinson Jeffers, in *The Criterion Book of Modern American Verse*.

Geoffrey Johnson, *A Man of Vision and Other Poems,* Robert Hale, Ltd., London, 1958.

Le Roi Jones, *Preface to a Twenty Volume Suicide Note,* Totem Press in association with Corinth Books, New York, 1961.

K. J. Kennedy, *Nude Descending a Staircase,* Doubleday & Co., Garden City, N.Y., 1961.

Plowden Kernan, in *Wings, A Quarterly of Verse,* Vol. X, No. 2, Summer, 1951.

Richard Kinney, in *Wings, A Quarterly of Verse,* Vol. XI, No. 3, Autumn, 1953.

Watson Kirkconnell, *Centennial Tales and Selected Poems,* University of Toronto Press, Toronto, 1965.

Maxine W. Kumin, *Poems,* Holt, Rinehart & Winston, New York, 1961.

Alexa Lane, in *Wings, A Quarterly of Verse,* Vol. I, No. 3, Autumn, 1933.

William Ellery Leonard, *Two Lives,* W. B. Huebsch, Inc., New York, 1925.

C. Day Lewis, in *The Pocket Book of Modern Verse.*

C. S. Lewis, *Poems,* edited by Walter Hooper, Harcourt, Brace & World, New York, 1965.

Vachel Lindsay, *Selected Poems,* edited by Mark Harris, The Macmillan Company, New York, 1963.

Jack London, in *Jack London, American Rebel,* A Collection of His Social Writings, edited by Philip S. Foner, The Citadel Press, New York, 1947.

Pare Lorentz, in *The Pocket Companion.*

Adelaide Love, in *Wings, A Quarterly of Verse,* Vol. XI, No. 3, Autumn, 1953.

Robert Lowell, *For the Union Dead,* Farrar, Straus and Giroux, New York, 1964.

———, *Life Studies,* Farrar, Straus and Cudahy, New York, 1959.

Archibald MacLeish, *Collected Poems, 1917–1952,* Houghton Mifflin Company, Boston, 1952.

Louis MacNeice, *Collected Poems, 1925–1948,* Faber & Faber, Ltd., London, 1949.

Claude McKay, in *The Book of American Negro Poetry.*

Edwin Markham, *Poems,* selected and arranged by Charles L. Wallis, Harper & Bros., New York, 1950.

John Masefield, *Old Raiger and Other Verse,* The Macmillan Company, New York, 1965.

———, *Poems,* complete edition with recent poems, The Macmillan Company, 1947.

Edgar Lee Masters, *Domesday Book,* The Macmillan Company, New York, 1920.

———, *Spoon River Anthology,* The Macmillan Company, 1915.

Eve Merriam, in Joy Davidman's *War Poems of the United Nations.*

Robert Mezey, *The Lovemaker,* Cummington Press, Iowa City, Iowa, 1961.

Edna St. Vincent Millay, *Collected Poems,* Harper & Bros., New York, 1945.

Minnie Hite Moody, in *Wings, A Quarterly of Verse,* Vol. XI, No. 1, Spring, 1953.

Marianne Moore, *Collected Poems,* The Macmillan Company, New York, 1951.

———, *What Are Years,* The Macmillan Company, 1941.

Merrill Moore, *Poems of American Life,* with Introduction by Louis Untermeyer, Philosophical Library, New York, 1958.

———, *Verse-Diary of a Psychiatrist,* Contemporary Poetry, Baltimore, 1954.

Barbara Moraff, in *Four Young Lady Poets,* Totem Press in association with Corinth Books, New York, 1962.

Robert Morse, *The Two Persephones,* Creative Age Press, New York, 1942.

David Morton, *Ships in Harbour,* G. P. Putnam's Sons, New York, 1921.

W. R. Moses, *Identities,* Wesleyan University Press, Middleton, Conn., 1965.

Edwin Muir, *Collected Poems, 1921–1951,* The Grove Press, New York, 1957.

Robert Nathan, *The Green Leaf, Collected Poems,* Alfred A. Knopf, New York, 1950.

Howard Nemerov, *Mirrors and Windows: Poems,* University of Chicago Press, Chicago, 1960.

———, *New and Selected Poems,* University of Chicago Press, 1958.

Louise Townsend Nicholl, *Collected Poems,* E. P. Dutton & Company, New York, 1953.

————, *Life in the Flesh*, E. P. Dutton & Company, 1947.

Charles Norman, *Selected Poems*, The Macmillan Company, New York, 1962.

Harold Norse, *The Dancing Beasts*, The Macmillan Company, New York, 1962.

Alfred Noyes, *Collected Poems in One Volume*, J. B. Lippincott Company, Philadelphia and New York, 1947.

Charles Olson, *Proprioception, Writing 6*, Four Seasons Foundation, San Francisco, 1965.

Arthur O'Shaughnessy, *Poems*, selected and edited by William Alexander Percy, Yale University Press, New Haven, 1923.

Wilfred Owen, *Poems*, with a Memoir and Notes by Edmund Blunden, The New Classics Series, Great Britain, 1949.

Sylvia Plath, *Ariel*, Harper & Row, New York, 1966.

Ezra Pound, *Cantos*, New Directions, New York, 1948.

————, *Selected Poems*, 4th ed., New Directions, 1962.

E. J. Pratt, *Collected Poems*, 2nd ed., with Introduction by Northrup Frye, The Macmillan Company of Canada, Toronto, 1958.

A. G. Prys-Jones, *Poems of Wales*, D. Appleton & Company, New York, 1924.

Howard Ramsden, in *Wings, A Quarterly of Verse*, Vol. VI, No. 5, Spring, 1944.

John Crowe Ransom, *Selected Poems*, Alfred A. Knopf, New York, 1945.

Lizette Woodworth Reese, *Selected Poems*, George H. Doran Company, New York, 1926.

Kenneth Rexroth, *Natural Numbers*, New and Selected Poems, New Directions, New York, 1963.

Cale Young Rice, *Best Poetic Work*, Cumberland University Press, Lebanon, Tenn., 1943.

E. V. Rieu, *The Tryst and Other Poems*, Oxford University Press, London, 1917.

Edwin Arlington Robinson, *Selected Poems*, edited by Morton Dwight Zabel, The Macmillan Company, New York, 1965.

Paul Roche, *The Rank Obstinacy of Things*, Sheed & Ward, New York, 1962.

Theodore Roethke, *The Far Field*, Doubleday & Company, Garden City, N.Y., 1964.

————, *Words for the Wind*, Doubleday & Co., Garden City, N.Y., 1958.

James Rorty, in *Poetry Awards, 1952*.

Muriel Rukuyser, *Body of Waking*, Harper & Bros., New York, 1958.

Lady Margaret Sackville, in *Harp Aeolian*, edited by Georgina Somerville, Burrows Press, Ltd., Cheltenham, England, n.d.

Carl Sandburg, *Chicago Poems*, Henry Holt & Company, New York, 1916.

Siegfried Sassoon, *Collected Poems*, The Viking Press, New York, 1949.

David Schubert, *Initial A*, The Macmillan Company, New York, 1961.

Delmore Schwartz, *Summer Knowledge, New and Selected Poems, 1938–1958*, Doubleday & Company, Garden City, N.Y., 1959.

Karl Shapiro, *The Bourgeois Poet*, Random House, New York, 2nd printing, 1964.

————, *An Essay on Rime*, Reynal & Hitchcock, New York, 1945.

Louis Simpson, "Love and Poetry," *Book Week*, November 13, 1966.

Edith Sitwell, *Gardeners and Astronomers*, The Vanguard Press, Inc., New York, 1953.

Clark Ashton Smith, *The Hill of Dionysius*, Pacific Grove, Calif., 1962.

W. D. Snodgrass, in *American Poetry*.

William Stafford, *Traveling Through the Dark*, Harper & Row, New York, 1962.

Victor S. Starbuck, *Saul, King of Israel*, The University of North Carolina Press, Chapel Hill, 1938

George Sterling, *Selected Poems*, A. M. Robertson, San Francisco, 1923.

Wallace Stevens, *Collected Poems*, Alfred A. Knopf, New York, 1964.

Adrien Stoutenburg, *Heroes, Advise Us*, Charles Scribner's Sons, New York, 1964.

May Swenson, *A Cage of Spines*, Rinehart & Company, New York, 1958.

Dylan Thomas, *Collected Poems*, New Directions, New York, 1957.

————, *New Poems*, New Directions, Norfolk, Conn., 1943.

Gilbert Thomas, *Later Poems*, David & Charles, Ltd., Dawlish, England, 1960.

Ridgely Torrence, *Poems, New Edition with New Poems*, The Macmillan Company, New York, 1952.

Philip Toynbee, *Two Brothers, The Fifth Day of the Valediction of Pantaloon*, Harper & Row, New York, 1964.

Frederick Goddard Tuckerman, *Complete Poems,* edited by M. Scott Momaday, with a Critical Foreword by Ivor Winters, Oxford University Press, 1965.

Joseph Upper, in *Wings, A Quarterly of Verse,* Vol. II, No. 5, Spring, 1936.

Constance Urdang, *Charades and Celebrations,* October House, Inc., New York, 1965.

John Wain, *A Carved Word on a Sill,* Routledge & Kegal Paul, London, 1956.

Theodore Weiss, *Outlanders,* The Macmillan Company, New York, 1960.

Philip Whalen, in *The New American Poetry.*

John Hall Wheelock, *Poems Old and New,* Charles Scribner's Sons, New York, 1956.

Thomas Whitbread, *Four Infinities,* Harper & Row, New York, 1964.

Edward Lucas White, *The Song of the Sirens and Other Stories,* E. P. Dutton & Co., New York, 1919.

Margaret Widdemer, *The Dark Cavalier, Collected Poems,* Doubleday & Company, Garden City, N.Y., 1958.

Lionel Wiggam, *The Land of Unloving,* The Macmillan Company, New York, 1961.

Richard Wilbur, *Things of This World,* Harcourt, Brace & Company, New York, 1956.

William Carlos Williams, *The Desert Music and Other Poems,* Random House, New York, 1955.

———, *Paterson,* New Directions, New York, 1963.

Harold Witt, *Beasts in Clothes,* The Macmillan Company, New York, 1961.

Helen Wolfert, *Nothing Is a Wonderful Thing,* Simon & Schuster, New York, 1946.

David Wright, in Brinnin and Read's *The Modern Poets.*

Louis Zukofsky, in *A Controversy of Poets.*

INDEX

Freedom in poetry, 138, 164, 172–90, 211–12, 221. *See also* Innovation; specific aspects, poets, works

Freund, Otto, 219

"From Homage to Mistress Bradstreet," 42

Frost, Robert, 9, 179, 182

Frost (Robert) Fellowship in Poetry, 75

"Garden of Proserpine, The," 212

Geometrical arrangement of lines, 36–37, 85. *See also* Form and arrangement; Punctuation

"Gerontion," 127–28

Gibran, Kahlil, 53–54

Gibson, Wilfred W., 125–26, 216

Gibson, William, 41

"Gift, A," 63–64

Gill, Katie May, 73

Ginsberg, Allen, 103–5

"God's World," 118–19

Golden Goose Chap Book, 39–40

Golden Treasury of Scottish Poetry, 163

Goldsmith, Oliver, 99

Goodman, Mae Winkler, 195

Gould, Gerald, 215

Graves, Robert, 121

Gray, Thomas, 10, 152, 209

Greco, El, 210

Greece and the Greeks, 15, 24. *See also* specific individuals, works

Gregory, Horace, 66–67, 188, 189

Grieve, Christopher Murray, 162–63

"Guest, The," 202–3

Guggenheim Memorial Fellowship, 17, 202

Guiterman, Arthur, 180

Hagedorn, Hermann, 119, 178, 180, 183

"Hairbrush, The," 41

Halfway, 36

Hall, Donald, 18

"Halley's Comet," 194–95

Hamlet, 208

Hamilton, Marion Ethel, 187

Harding, Ruth F., 180, 187

Hardy, Thomas, 120, 174, 215

"Harlem Dancer, The," 107

"Harper's Ferry Floating Away," 93

Harper's Magazine, 38

"Harry Ploughman," 59

Hartsock (Ernest) Memorial Prize, 17

Hassell, Christopher, 214

Hawk in the Rain, The, 42

Hearn, Lafcadio, 21

Hedley, Leslie Woolf, 79

"Hellas," 200

Herrick, Robert, 142

Hesketh, Phoebe, 216

"Hesperian Fall," 186

Heywood, Terence, 35

Hicky, Daniel W., 180

Hillyer, Robert, 180, 183

Hines, Carl Wendell, 103

Hirschmann, Jack, 97

Hodgson, William Noel, 197–98

Holbrook, David, 11

Holmes, Daris, 97

Holmes, John, 167

THE AUTHOR AND HIS BOOK

STANTON A. COBLENTZ was born in San Francisco in 1896. He attended the University of California at Berkeley and received his master's degree in English in 1919.

During his long and prolific career as a writer and poet, Mr. Coblentz has produced twelve science-fiction novels, eighteen volumes of poetry, five poetry anthologies, and several other books, including *From Arrow to Atom Bomb, The Long Road to Humanity, Demons, Witch Doctors and Modern Man, Ten Crises in Civilization,* and *The Paradox of Man's Greatness.* Among his books about poetry are *An Editor Looks at Poetry* and *The Rise of the Anti-Poets.*

From 1933 to 1960 Mr. Coblentz was editor of *Wings, A Quarterly of Verse.* He has contributed numerous free-lance feature articles and book reviews to the San Francisco *Chronicle,* the San Francisco *Examiner, The New York Times,* the New York *Sun,* and other leading newspapers.

Mr. Coblentz is married and lives in Mill Valley, California.

THE POETRY CIRCUS was composed, printed and bound by the H. Wolff Book Manufacturing Co. of New York City. The text is set in Granjon, the most popular type face of the Garamond group.

A HAWTHORN BOOK